THE MATINEE IDOLS

DAVID CARROLL

THE MATINEE IDOLS

ARBOR HOUSE
NEW YORK

I wish to thank the following for pictures and assistance:
20th Century-Fox
MGM Studios
United Artists
Paramount Pictures
Warner Brothers
Republic Studios
Columbia Pictures
The Walter Hampden Memorial Library at The Players, New York
The Lincoln Center Library for the Performing Arts
Mr. James Martin
Mr. George Lambert
Mr. and Mrs. Sidney Carroll
Photographics, Florida, New York
Mr. Douglas Homs (*technical assistance*)
Mr. Louis A. Rachow
Mr. Carl Willers
and with special thanks and gratitude to
Mr. Griffin Crafts

Library of Congress Catalog Card Number: 72-184882
ISBN 0-87795-031-8

MANUFACTURED IN THE UNITED STATES OF AMERICA
Designed by Bob Antler

FOR MY FATHER

CONTENTS

Introduction

PART ONE: THE THEATER

Edmund Kean: *The Pre-Matinee Matinee Idol,* 27

John Wilkes Booth: *The Mad Matinee Idol,* 31

Harry Montague: *The First Matinee Idol,* 35

Kyrle Bellew: *The Reluctant Matinee Idol,* 40

Charles Fechter: *The French Matinee Idol,* 45

Frank Mayo: *The Matinee Idol Despite Himself,* 46

Maurice Barrymore: *The Swaggering Matinee Idol,* 49

The Matinee Ladies, 52

Chauncey Olcott: *The Singing Matinee Idol,* 59

Henry Dixie: *The Funny Matinee Idol,* 62

Wilton Lackaye: *The Horrifying Matinee Idol,* 65

James J. Corbett: *The Athlete-Turned-Matinee Idol,* 68

Robert Mantell: *The Emotive Matinee Idol,* 70

John Drew: *The Drawing Room Matinee Idol,* 72

James K. Hackett: *The Cape and Sword Matinee Idol,* 76

Henry Miller: *The Gentle Matinee Idol,* 79

William Faversham: *The Decline of the Matinee Idol,* 80

PART TWO: FILM

Francis X. Bushman: *The First Matinee Idol of Film,* 85

Lou Tellegen: *The Continental Matinee Idol,* 91

Douglas Fairbanks: *The Patriotic Matinee Idol,* 96

William S. Hart and Tom Mix:
The Western Matinee Idol, 107

Wallace Reid: *The All-American Matinee Idol,* 113

Rudolph Valentino: *The Exotic Matinee Idol,* 122

Ramon Novarro: *The Second Exotic Matinee Idol,* 132

John Gilbert: *The Public Loves of the Matinee Idol,* 139

John Barrymore: *The Last Matinee Idol,* 145

The Demise of the Matinee Idol, 153

INTRODUCTION

A matinee idol is a male entertainer whose appeal is primarily to the female sex. He need not be an Adonis nor even an especially handsome man, although he is usually both. It is not requisite that he be a dramatic genius; as a matter of fact, it really doesn't matter if he can act at all. What *is* requisite is that he be able to whisper to the hearts of women, and to their libidos, in a voice that says "I am I; I attract you; never mind what I say or do, I am here before you and you cannot, no matter how hard you try, avoid me."

It is thus visceral and emotional attractions which make a matinee idol, as it is these qualities which separate him from other actors. Women laughed at John Bunny and Harold Lloyd, were awed by the artistry of Edwin Booth, marveled at the suavity of George Arliss, were intimidated by the bearlike power of Lionel Barrymore, but none of these men qualified as matinee idols because none of them evoked passion. And if some of the performers who did arouse women were at the same time magnificent actors, men like Edmund Kean and John Barrymore, who were as talented as Ramon Novarro or Kyrle Bellew were not, well and good; they were matinee idols who could act as well.

The matinee idol was a woman's creation. Men occasionally attended a matinee and no doubt helped the idol's career by imitating him when they returned home, but the man's place in making male darlings was still a small one. Matinees were tailored for the female mentality; and besides, the men were busy—they were at work.

Needless to say, it would be convenient for our story if we

could state that the term "matinee idol" came into creation on such and such an afternoon when nine women jumped out of the balcony onto the stage, causing a wag in the pits to coin the term. Unfortunately this information is not available, and we can only guess how the term originated. Some say it was invented in the West End of London where melodramatic male performers could be viewed each midday dueling and wooing their way across the stage in whatever drama was popular that week with the ladies. William Brady, the American producer, however, claims it was an American invention, created to describe Harry Montague, who in 1875 was the first Apollolike lead to appear when matinees were just becoming popular.

The word "matinee" itself derives from the French *matin*, meaning morning, and was introduced into English in 1848 in the novel *Vanity Fair* when Thackeray mentioned a "*matinée* musical." But more than sixty years would pass until the acute accent was dropped and the word became an unitalicized part of the language. Through some imponderable transaction during this naturalization process, the meaning of the word in theatrical usage also changed, and by the time of the Civil War a matinee was a performance given between the hours of one and two o'clock.

An early advertisement for a matinee.

Immediately after the Civil War, matinees became current in America (although they didn't catch on in England until a famous theatrical family named Bancroft gave regular one o'clock showings of Sardou's *Diplomacy* in 1879), and we may assume that somewhere in the twenty-five years following that war the term "matinee idol" originated.

But if the phrase was not in use until the third quarter of the nineteenth century, the phenomenon it expressed had for many years been part of the American theatrical picture. Even by the beginning of the nineteenth century managers chose plays less on the grounds of their dramatic merit than on the charm and personality of the principal actors who, if they possessed enough appeal, could keep the most insipid drama on the boards for many weeks. Indeed, since 1800 and before, certain Shakespearean actors had been singled out and lionized by the public, and by 1820 in America the great English actor, Edmund Kean, was a far more illustrious drawing card than Shakespeare himself.

Kean, like other actors of his time, enjoyed the fruits of the "star system" which was just becoming conspicuous. Before 1800 the play itself was the main attraction and actors were simply mechanics trained to give it entertaining expression. As a result, each theater had its own resident company staffed with versatile performers familiar with dozens of plays and capable of playing three or four parts in each. But in the early part of the nineteenth century it became apparent that the populace responded more to the actor than to the play. Slowly, those individuals in the repertory groups who especially appealed to the masses were elevated above their peers and given separate billing. Soon they became stars and as such they became mobile as well, appearing with the rep companies of different theaters throughout the east. By 1835 the star system was in full swing.

It was not without its faults. Managers became convinced that their only chance for success was to procure big names, and they hired stars at enormous salaries. If the production then laid an egg they might easily go bankrupt. More insidiously, with the majority of available revenues channeled toward the star, members of the stock company took salary cuts, and many talented repertory players began to leave the stage in search of more lucrative professions. William Wood was one of those to feel the squeeze. "The star is the light of everything," wrote the actor in 1855, "the center about which all must move. He has his own time, his own pieces, his own plan of business and his own preferences of every sort. One star is very tall and will play with no person of diminutive stature. The company must be changed to suit him. The next is very short and will play with no one of ordinary height. Everything is again to be unsettled. One star brings half a company with him and the stock actors, thus displaced, retire in disappointment."

Before long the best of the repertory actors had departed, leaving such abysmal second-stringers to replace them that visiting stars sometimes brought two or three actors with them to fill key roles. This caught on, and by 1880 "combination companies" were the rule, entire troupes of performers who toured with their own props, scenery, cast, and of course, the inevitable star. It was expensive to procure new flats and costumes for each different play, however, so stars began specializing in one or two roles alone, sometimes playing the same part for many years, and they gained reputations as certain kinds of actors—as comedians, villains, tragedians, and of course, as matinee idols.

In the later part of the century the star system was accelerated to its ultimate conclusions by Charles Frohman, a stout little autocrat from Sandusky, Ohio, who began his career as a cigar salesman and ended it known as "Napoleon of the Drama." His star-making method was direct and highly effective. He called it "instant elevation." Before his time it had taken actors years of apprenticeship and privation to become established. But why was this necessary, asked Frohman? Why not use modern advertising to speed up the procedure a little? Why not "make" a star, create him from scratch, and why waste time in the process? To put this plan into operation he amassed ten thousand employees whom he paid over thirty-five million dollars a year, and deployed hundreds of scouts to canvass the sticks for talent. When they found this talent they brought it to him and he methodically set about selling it to the public. Having founded most of the American booking offices himself, it was no trick to get a new face he was pushing placed in a leading role. Then came the publicity releases, the pictures in the papers, the interviews, the endorsements, the phony scandals —in short, all the tricks of modern publicity. From 1885 to 1914, using these force-feeding tactics on theatergoers, Charles Frohman promoted more than fifty performers to stardom, and in 1915, when a German torpedo sent him to his death on the *Lusitania,* he left Broadway with a controversial legacy, the commercializing and big-businessizing of the American theater.

The star syndrome was obviously the most fertile soil for the growth of the matinee idol and predictably, by 1890, his proliferation was considered an epidemic by those who supported the repertory tradition. Supporters of the old regime were not only peeved by the fact that many of these "two-week wonders" were hams of the first water; they were also affronted by the type of plays they popularized—superficial, crowd-pleasing thrillers that through an odd twist of semantics had come to be called "melodramas" (originally a melodrama was a passage in German opera in which the hero remained silent and allowed the music to express his feelings).

Stage Heroine.

The Stage Hero.

So stereotyped did melodrama become that the writer, Jerome K. Jerome, was prompted to satirize the whole predictable syndrome. He wrote:

"The stage hero never talks in a simple, straightforward way, like a mere ordinary mortal.

" 'You will write to me when you are away, Dear, wont you?' says the heroine.

"A mere human being would reply, 'Why of course, Ducky, every day.'

"But the stage hero is a superior creature. He says, 'Dos't see yonder star, sweet?'

"She looks up and owns that she does see yonder star and there off he starts and drivels on about the star for full five minutes, and says he will cease to write her when the star has fallen from its place amidst the firmament of Heaven.

"The heroine, however, is always in trouble—and don't she let you know it, too. Her life is undeniably a hard one. Nothing goes right for her. We all have our troubles, but the stage heroine never has anything else. If she only got one afternoon a week off from troubles, or had her Sundays free it would be something, but no! Misfortune stalks beside her from week's beginning to week's end."

Melodrama was a perfect medium for the beautiful but untalented actor, an ingenious invention that used action-packed stories and heaps of candied romance to conceal the idol's inability to act. It stressed action at the expense of characterization, moralized in a black-and-white fashion, was improbable, lachrymose, thrilling, and inevitably romantic. The central characters were the hero, heroine, and villain, supported by other predictables such as the saucy soubrette, the beloved father, the busybody maid, the jolly Irishman, the comic, and the attorney. The situations centered on a hundred variations of the villain's attempts to befuddle the heroine, and the hero's attempts to foil him. All of this took place before picturesque and sometimes amazingly elaborate sets, ranging from the jungles of Borneo to the drawing room of Madame X.

MR. EDWIN BEVERLEY.
Intense Parts.
SHAKESPEAREAN & MODERN.

STRONG CHARACTER LEADS.
EMOTIONAL ACTING.
Address, care of " The Stage."

Some matinee idols, like Mr. Beverley, advertised. One can scarcely blame him. Stage love-making was big business, and competitive as well.

Primarily an American invention, melodramas became popular both here and in England when matinees were becoming common. They were an outgrowth of the "romantic drama" which was born in early nineteenth-century France as a protest against the classic school, gone stale. Romantic drama combined the English Gothic motifs of subterranean passageways, raving lovers in haunted castles, and ghouls on the moors, with Italian lyricism, German romanticism à la Goethe, and the French cavalier tradition. Alexandre Dumas *fils* was one leader of this movement, Victor Hugo another, and Guilbert de Pixerécourt, one of the earliest blood-and-thunder dramatists of the day, a third. So gluttonous did French appetites for romantic drama become that Dumas built a playhouse called the Théâtre Historique for the performances of the plays he had written, such as *The Three Musketeers* and *The Count of Monte Cristo*, but soon the walls of the playhouse could not contain the appeal of the romantic drama and it traveled across the sea to the New World, where it was sensationalized, emotionalized, and thoroughly americanized as melodrama.

It was the arrival of the matinee, the star system, and the

melodrama which created the matinee idol. The matinee furnished the time and the place, the melodrama provided the vehicle, and stardom brought the people. By 1900 the idol was as firmly established in the American theater as the ticket office, and to his backstage doorway came hundreds of palpitating, breast-heaving females who cornered him like wolves surrounding a stag, some reaching out to stroke his coat, his shoes, anything; others standing planted to the earth on which he walked, in mute adulation. To these women everything their idols did, everything they read, ate, thought, or spoke was a matter of supreme importance. They made demigods of these men by attributing to them all the virtues of the characters they played. And although it was part of the idol's role to feign bored indifference to this admiration, he was nevertheless quite aware that his job depended on these women, and played up to them offstage, gave interviews and autographs, modeled for ads in provocative poses, and wrote teasing articles on such profound subjects as "Why I Like Women Who Wear Hats," or "What a Matinee Man Likes for Breakfast."

A matinee girl of the 1880's.

As the numbers of female theatergoers multiplied, new phrases were coined to describe their idiosyncrasies. A "matinee hat" was a large, flowery bonnet, notorious for blocking people's views. Newspaper articles devoted to starry-eyed stage gossip were called "gush columns." The "rush seats," located in front row center, afforded a close-up view of celebrities, and women "rushed" to get them. When a young girl was absent from school because of "idolitis," she was really swooning in the galleries. "Mashers" were male idols and "mash letters" were love notes written to them, sometimes containing proposals of marriage or out-and-out propositions. "Matinee money" was the allowance a husband gave his wife for the week's groceries and which she spent otherwise at the theater, and "Matinee Millies," "Matinee Marthas," and "Matinee Madames" were all familiar terms of mild opprobrium for ladies who passed many of their daylight hours at the drama.

But the best known of all these terms was the "matinee girl." The matinee girl was the one who went to see the matinee idol. She was the not-too-distant relative of the bobby-soxer and could be found in droves at any local theater. So quickly populated did her ranks become that *Theatre* magazine devoted whole articles to dressing her down. "The matinee girl who makes herself conspicuous," it wrote in 1903, "is to be seen at all the

Sheet music from Donald Brian's biggest hit of 1913, The Marriage Market.

theaters, but is preeminent at the popular priced ones. Sometimes she is at the adorable age of early twenties and then it is hard to forgive her; much oftener, however, she is at the nuisance age of the middle teens. Usually she is in bunches, two or three in a crowd, and invariably she is noisy. All through the play one hears such snatches of conversation as: 'Isn't he just darling?'; 'I think he's the most handsome man I ever saw'; 'It must be grand to be an actress.'

"And one wonders what kind of mothers these girls have who not only permit schoolgirls to wear exaggerations in style, but to behave with rudeness and inconsideration to the people who want to hear an actor."

"It is hard work to be a beauty," Lillian Russell once said, and the same was true of being a matinee idol. The matinee girls were just one of the annoyances involved in the love business. Donald Brian, a glamorous singer of the early 1900's, had his troubles like the rest. "The matinee idol may walk or take a car," he wrote, "but not in peace. Someone is sure to recognize him, and with the curious belief of the public's that celebrities lack the senses of sight and hearing, make audible remarks: 'I don't like him in the part'; 'He can't sing. Why does he try?'; 'He's not so handsome off the stage'; 'If you ask me I think he's rotten.' "

The life of the idol was a ceaseless struggle to live up to his own lithographs. Occasionally, by taking good care of himself, one of them might remain a romantic star for ten or twenty years, playing loverboy even when a paunch obtruded over his waistcoat and his knees cracked when he kneeled. "A man never knew when he was too old to play Romeo," John Barrymore once remarked. "In the old days in the theater an aged Romeo was not infrequent. He may have looked like a corseted bloodhound, but he carried his lifted face proudly." Most, however, when middle-aged spread or a new competitor appeared, were deserted by a fickle female following whose loyalties were as ephemeral as bubbles. The matinee idol, for all his pomp and beauty, bloomed but for a day.

A peep show parlor, the dirty bookstores of their time.

For fifty years the stage idol was king supreme of virgin hearts, but one sad day in the early years of the twentieth century he was deposed swiftly and surely by the motion pictures.

In the beginning there were no stars, no studios, not even a screen. There were only Kinetoscopes, better known to those members of the lower establishment who frequented them as "peep shows." In 1898 this riffraff paid their coins to enter the dingy, ill-ventilated penny arcades and crank the arms of "Edison's latest amazing invention." Before their astounded eyes appeared such phantasmagoric wonders as a bird flying through the air, a wave breaking on the shore, or the sneeze of a pedestrian-looking middle-aged man. Yet it is difficult for us to comprehend just how remarkable all this must have seemed to the turn-of-the-century mentality, not yet jaded by assembly-line production wonders, especially when these pictures were finally passed through the magic lantern and projected onto a screen. People reached out to touch them, tried to talk to them, screamed in horror when the images of locomotives and falling trees headed in their direction. They moved! And of their own accord! Moving shadows on a strip of celluloid.

For a time audiences were satisfied with these flickering, prosaic splendors of sternutation and Mother Nature. No one really cared if they were dull or even if they contained no people at all; it was miracle enough that they were there in the first place. But even the most astounding novelties become trite through overexposure, and by 1900 it looked as if moving pictures would be just what Edison and his cohorts had dismissed them as—useless toys. Soon films were shown in burlesque houses between strips or after the last act in vaudeville shows while people filed out of the theater. It was this early association with such lowbrow amusements, as well as the unsavory atmosphere of the early theaters, called nickel-odeons, which kept films in bad odor for so many years.

Then in 1901 a Frenchman named Georges Méliès decided that the way to make films interesting was the way to make anything interesting: tell a story. In his mad scientist's laboratory in the basement of his house (he was a professional magician by trade) he began turning out short, compact films (*Cinderella* in 1900, *Red Riding Hood* and *Bluebeard* in 1901), each a miniature feature. In 1903 an American named Edwin Porter picked up on this and brought the narrative film to America with *The Life of an American Fireman* and in 1905 *The Great Train Robbery*. The American film business was on its way.

Of course, if you were going to tell stories you needed people to tell them with, and the obvious choice fell to out-of-work stage performers. At five dollars and ten dollars a week it was a grueling way to make a living and seemed a degrading step down from the stage. Furthermore, the names of these early players were withheld from the public for the first few years of production, making it difficult for them to become established. The studios claimed this was done by law for the protection of the actors. But others knew better; once an actor became famous he also became expensive.

By 1908 the films were no longer a curiosity. There were six thousand nickelodeons in America with hundreds more opening each month. Once such theaters had been as dank as the penny arcades, but by 1910 these cramped little auditoriums with their camp chairs and pianos were transformed into plush theaters. Suddenly carpets, soft chairs, thick rugs, and small orchestras replaced the dilapidated nickelodeons, and prices rose accordingly. Films were here to stay.

Arthur Johnson

Maurice Costello

The early silents, however, were rooted in the tradition of the theater. It couldn't be otherwise. Almost all the original film performers were from the stage, as were the directors, producers, and even the prop men and set designers. Melodramas and classic plays were the common vehicles, and techniques of performing were straight from old-time drama. Players acted with their bodies, with their chins, with their rolling eyes and stamping feet, with elaborate gestures and exaggerated facial expressions. Behind them were sets as realistic as those used for "melothrillers," but they were still just sets. It rarely occurred to anyone to shoot a film on location.

Stage direction was also out of the 1890's. Action took place in the center of the screen, as if the screen were a stage. Actors stood in self-consciously arranged groups. Everything was filmed in long shots (the close-up came later with D. W. Griffith), and the performers walked stiffly back and forth on cue. But what had worked so well on stage now seemed strangely inappropriate. It was the right direction applied to the wrong medium.

The matinee performance was also part of the carry-over from theater to films, and the word "matinee," like Bijou or Embassy, became a common name for early movie theaters. It was not long before the matinee idol too would have his name in lights. By 1908 millions of Americans had become addicted to motion pictures, and they exerted enormous pressure on the studios to find out the names of certain film actors. Who was the wavy-haired cowboy? Who was the blonde with the curls? Who was the lean-faced melancholy collegiate type? Who was the IMP Girl? (IMP was the name of her studio.) That year Carl Laemmle, founder of Universal Pictures, announced that the IMP Girl was really Florence Lawrence. Shortly thereafter other studios started giving out such data and the star system of the films was born.

It turned out that the girl with curls was Mary Pickford, the wavy-haired buckeroo was Billy Anderson, and the melancholy collegiate was Arthur Johnson.

Arthur Johnson then became the screen's first matinee idol. By profession a Shakespearean actor, he had spent many years barnstorming with Robert Mantell and came to the Lubin studios in 1907. There he joined Florence Lawrence in a number of one-reel romances and they became the first popular romantic couple in films. With her and without her he became the object of many young women's affections. His daredevil stunts, his leaps off moving trains, and his broad jumps over chasms predated Fairbanks by seven

D. W. Griffith gives Lillian Gish some last minute instructions while two of his male stars, Tom Moore (second from left) and Bobby Harron (leaning on the desk) look on.

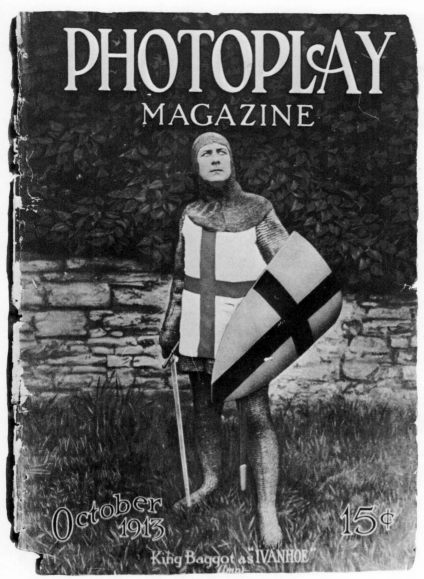

King Baggot

years, and his square-chinned, aristocratic face gave him the plastic perfection that people adored. His career as the first idol, however, was brief. By 1915 he had quit films and was occupied thereafter with drinking himself to death.

Henry B. Walthall with Theda Bara in East Lynne. *Courtesy, 20th Century-Fox.*

Next to Johnson, the most popular idol of the early screen was Maurice Costello. Costello had been on the stage for more than twenty years and by the time his film career began he was well over forty. The appeal of the middle-aged man, however, the man who had "lived," was more in evidence at that time than it is today, and for a few years Costello got away with it. Eventually his age became embarrassingly apparent and even intensified advertising slogans, billing him as a "mature actor," no longer seemed anything but transparent euphemisms.

Other new names began to appear in print and on people's

lips: King Baggot, Henry B. Walthall, Tom Moore, Bobby Harron, J. Warren Kerrigan, Carlyle Blackwell; and to theater people it was clear that these men were pulling customers away from the theaters. "The idolatry that the matinee idol inspired has been destroyed by the actor of new adventures, the film man," wrote Charles Cherry, an old matinee idol himself. "He has entirely replaced the stage idol, immensely enlarged his zone of romantic influence and created a state of idolatry quite inexplicable to any previous human psychology."

But in truth the great age of the screen matinee idol had not yet begun. It wouldn't start until 1911, when a young square-shouldered man named Francis X. Bushman came to Essanay Film

Francis X. Bushman with Beverly Bayne in The Great Secret *made in 1917.*

Studios and started making movies. He would provide the impetus that allowed the matinee idol to survive for another decade in the new medium of the silent screen.

The story of all our matinee idols—both stage and screen—actually begins in the early nineteenth century when a certain British actor toured the United States. He was not conventionally handsome, nor was he quite a matinee idol in the modern sense of the word. But he was the first of the great romantic actors to come to this country and the first to have an appeal to women that was dramatically reflected in their public behavior. His name was Edmund Kean.

PART ONE

THE THEATER

The Pre-Matinee Matinee Idol

EDMUND KEAN

In the year 1814 the streets of London and Paris were populated with strange beings, "youthful barbarians" the gazettes called them, all in their early twenties and fitted out in shoulder-length hair, enormous Rubens hats, velvet pantaloons, and *cahiers* full of nostalgic verses. "Life is lyrical, not logical," they cried. "Feelings come before facts, art is higher than science, nature is greater than the machine, and the ordinary man, the common man, must be given his due."

The age of romanticism had arrived.

Edmund Kean as Richard III, the role that created riots for and against Kean at American theaters.

But the ordinary man and the common man, despite the attempts of the reformers, still remained ordinary and still remained common, and it was clear that a shift in emphasis was required. "Creative individualism," they then shouted, "creative individualism above all else. *Vive l'artiste!*" and off they dashed to the ateliers, to the concert halls and sculptors' studios, and especially to the theaters, where they originated an institution which is still in favor today, the reign of the solitary above the diverse, the one above the many, the single personality—the star.

On the evening of January 26, 1814, when the clamor for famous dramaticians was just beginning in London, a young man named Edmund Kean was given the role of Shylock in *The Merchant of Venice*. Traditionally, Shylock was portrayed as an insensate monstrosity, and the small crowd of regulars in attendance at the Drury Lane Theater saw no reason to expect something new. But the age of humanism was upon Europe, and that night Kean made Shylock into a human being, a confused and persecuted little

Jewish moneylender, a man capable of real, if distorted, feelings. The audience watched in dazzled stupefaction as Shylock cried *real* tears. "Hath not a Jew eyes, hath not a Jew ears?" he asked, and the words took on a different meaning. At the end of the last act the house was on its feet in wild applause.

Word spread of this strange new actor who, it was said, gave the impression of *becoming* rather than *acting* the characters he played, and women began to crowd the galleries. When they had come to the theater at all they had come to see the play; now they came exclusively to see one man, to see Edmund Kean. It was not just the realism of his characterizations they liked; it was his sheer thunderous emotionality that fascinated them, an emotionality that lifted people out of their seats, caused painted dames in the twopenny rows to toss garters on stage and the demure ladies of the balcony to beat the air with their ivory fans in ever-increasing intensity. A night's performance of Kean's *Othello* seldom passed without at least one woman falling off her chair in a faint and being carried to the back of the auditorium for a whiff of smelling salts, and after seeing this *Othello* a playgoer remarked, "I saw those eyes all night." Contemporary Shakespeareans prided themselves on mellifluence of rhetoric, correctness of stance, precision of diction. But *real* feelings? *real* passions? *real* emotions? No one had even bothered to remember them until Kean appeared.

"To see Kean," said Samuel Taylor Coleridge, in the most famous remark ever made about an actor, "was to read Shakespeare by lightning."

The cult of personality had begun.

In 1820, when Kean was in his fullest bloom, he announced a tour of the United States, and the American theater, not yet weaned from its commercial dependence on the visits of British actors, prepared to make something large of it. The clamor to get tickets for his *Richard III* marked the first recorded instance of scalper's prices in America, and when the tickets sold out, riots shook the box offices. "The Kean fever," wrote William Clapp in *Record of the Boston Stage,* "broke and raged without cession. His acting was the all engrossing subject of fashionable discussion, and Kean himself became the lion of the day."

The tour was such an enormous success that Kean decided to extend its run for a few more nights in Boston. But by this time the theatrical season had been declared officially closed, and to the Bostonian's way of figuring this meant one simply didn't go to the

Kean as Othello. Benjamin West, the American painter, remarked that he had "never seen so much expression in any human face."

A contemporary British caricature of the Kean-Cox liaison, drawn, curiously enough, by an artist named Cox. The choleric gentleman seen through the window is the cuckold himself, Alderman Cox. The antlers crowning his brow are a symbol of adultery, whence comes the expression "horny."

theater. When only a handful of people came to the opening and when by the third night things got no better, Kean walked out on the performance, bringing on himself the ire of the whole city.

In 1825 he returned to America, this time hounded by news of his "criminal conversation" with a certain Mrs. Cox, the wife of a city alderman. The scandal became even more of a *cause célèbre* when the papers published his love letters to the alderman's wife, and by the time Kean arrived in America the blue-nosed press, already furious at him for the Boston incident, had its muskets drawn. They were repelled by this adulterer, they said, and they inflamed an already loaded situation by railing against the indecent applause he received from "women of the town, quantities of scum, ladies of the lobby, and wolves of the 'Coal-Hole.'" So horrendous did his press become that when he finally opened in *Richard III* at Boston's Park Theater, the audience pelted him into the wings with eggs and soft squashes, and as the evening progressed the scene turned into a free-for-all, with the hysterical participants ripping the seats out of the theater. Full-scale pandemonium finally took over and the whole thing ended with the destruction of the Park Theater and the great Kean, cast now in his least heroic role, fleeing for his life.

He returned to London and for eight more years struggled on against a waning reputation and a hostile press, destroying himself on alcohol as he sank into obscurity. While playing *Othello* in March of 1833 he collapsed halfway through the performance —it was his last—and two months later he was dead.

The first great romantic star of the English-speaking stage, Kean was also its first casualty; and as he lay dying, penniless and forgotten, it would, no doubt, have been scanty consolation for him to know he would assuredly not be the last.

An artist's depiction of the greeting Mr. Kean received from American audiences in 1825.

The Mad Matinee Idol

JOHN WILKES BOOTH

Despite his veritable expungement from the annals of theatrical history and despite the reluctance of authorities to mention it, the theater, after all, has never recovered from the fact that it was an actor who murdered Mr. Lincoln, and in a theater no less—John Wilkes Booth was in his time one of the great romantic figures of the stage.

Booth was a strange and melancholy man, prone, even as a child, to paranoid delusions and unaccountable obsessions. He loved and hated to unreasonable extremes, and so alienated his amiable brother, the great actor Edwin Booth, that they rarely spoke for the last ten years of John Booth's life. Yet the devil must be paid his due. Booth's contemporaries wrote that he was generous to a fault, a great wit, a liberal-hearted friend, and an extraordinarily handsome man. "Picture to yourself an Adonis," wrote Sir Charles Wyndham, "with high forehead, ascetic face corrected by rather full lips, sweeping black hair, a figure of perfect youthful proportions with the most wonderful black eyes in the world. Such was John Wilkes Booth."

• 31

John Wilkes Booth. "A man," said Sir Charles Wyndham, "of polished exterior, pleasing address, highly respectable in every regard, received into the best circles of society, his company sought after, exceedingly bold . . ."

He was likewise a performer of exceptional talent. When audiences saw him violently emote in Shakespearean parts ordinarily played with dispassionate rigidity, they compared him to Edmund Kean, and did so again when he interpreted Hamlet as a madman, bereft of faculties, drooling, frenzied, and deranged. Then, another evening, another play, and Booth became the Douglas Fairbanks of the 1860's. He rode horses across the proscenium, fell off cliffs, jumped into the audience, dueled with such ferocity that he often actually slashed and stabbed his opponents. He was the first to incorporate daredevil leaps and bounds into the romantic actor's vocabulary, and these stage-learned acrobatics helped him, no doubt, to make the seemingly impossible leap from Lincoln's box onto the stage the night of the shooting.

Twenty years before anyone had heard of a matinee idol, Booth was the recipient of a hundred love letters a week, was followed home by women, was carried off the stage by them, and was the first actor on record to have his clothes shredded by a gang of zealous fans. "Now it is scarcely an exaggeration," wrote the actress Clara Morris, "to say that the sex was in love with John Booth. At the theater, good heaven, as the sunflowers turn their stalks to follow the beloved sun, so old and young alike, our faces smiling, turned to him. And the letters from flirtatious women and alas! girls, you may believe were legion."

The great Edwin Booth (left), brother of John Wilkes Booth, most famous, perhaps, of all American Shakespeareans, and the Italian tragedian, Tommaso Salvini (right). Salvini once boasted he could reduce an audience to tears by reading them a menu. So popular were his blood-stirring histrionics that when he came to America and played Iago to Booth's Othello, thousands came to watch him although they knew in advance he would play the whole thing in Italian.

A sensationalized rendition of the assassination. The artist has taken a stage photograph of Booth, drawn in the president and his wife, and superimposed a gun and dagger not so neatly in Booth's hands. To the right the foul fiend, Lucifer, breathes evil instructions into the obsessed actor's ear and points the way to Lincoln's box. Booth's association with the theater helped him carry out the murder and contributed to his capture. "Whoever it was," wrote the New York Herald on April 15, 1865, "it is plainly evident that he thoroughly understood the theater and all the approaches and modes of escape . . . Miss Keene (who was on stage) said she recognized him as John Wilkes Booth, the actor . . ."

During the Civil War these febrile admirers unwittingly helped Booth to carry out secret missions for the Confederacy. Although he resided in Washington at this time, actors were granted diplomatic immunity and could move freely back and forth across the Mason-Dixon Line, an interesting comment on the powers of popular taste to transcend political hostilities. Booth was popular in north and south alike, and he toured the major cities of both. Posing as everybody's favorite leading man, he was all the while smuggling information to Jefferson Davis.

It was also Booth's reputation as a favorite actor that enabled him to get backstage of Ford's Theater the night of the assassination. He had played there before, knew most of the stagehands, and moments before he shot Lincoln had joked familiarly with the manager. No one would have dreamed of challenging his right to be there, even as he slowly edged his way to the off-limits section at the base of the staircase leading to the president's box.

"You sock-dologizing old man-trap," bellowed Harry Hawk, who was playing Asa Trenchard in *Our American Cousin,* and the roars of laughter almost drowned out the gunshot. Before the audience had come to its senses, a young man in a dark cape, brandishing a dagger in one hand and a smoking revolver in the other, leaped with a flourish onto the stage (it would have been a perfect jump, had he not tripped over an American flag), cried that the south had been avenged, and was gone. His high forehead and ascetic face, his rather full lips and sweeping black hair were

John Wilkes Booth, dying, carried out of the burning barn by federal troops.

his undoing. Theatergoers in the audience immediately recognized him and reported his name to the authorities. Twelve days later he lay dead outside a flaming barn in Virginia. Found on his body were the portraits of five beautiful women said to have been fans who sent him their pictures. Their names were never disclosed.

The First Matinee Idol

HARRY MONTAGUE

With the coming of Harry Montague to the American stage the era of the big-time matinee idol began. Before his arrival men like John Booth and Edmund Kean indeed were mobbed, but by relatively small groups and only on certain occasions. When Montague appeared, romance went public. It was the year 1878 and the Victorian ethic ruled. One of the few places people could legally go to vent their repressed spleens was the theater, traditionally neutral territory and, like the church in medieval times, a place of relative asylum from outside interference.

This does not mean that plays themselves were licentious; far from it, especially at this time. The license for uninhibitedness belonged to audiences, not actors. In pit or box seats, crowds could supersede Victorian injunctions—swear, hoot, cheer, pelt the stage with garbage, stand up and stretch in the middle of a play, have a fistfight, walk in or out at their discretion, eat their lunch, insult the actors, sob, laugh, and generally let themselves go in what was no doubt one of the most useful therapies of the period. This is why the outlandish matinee idol craze was permitted to exist at all in these times. At home the demure little lady would die before she raised her voice or eyed some good-looking young caller; but once safely within the theater, hidden in the dark amidst mobs of unrestrained women, she was at liberty, by tradition, to be herself.

Before Montague's time, however, theater was off-limits to unaccompanied women, especially at night. Any woman who ventured there alone was, *ipso facto,* a girl of easy virtue, and

Harry Montague, the first official matinee idol.

women either attended with their families and husbands or stayed at home.

But by the middle 1870's the matinees had arrived, and since they were presented at the respectable hour of one-thirty in the afternoon, women were free to patronize them alone. The result was that they started coming in enormous numbers, adolescents for the first time among them, and matinees sometimes played to houses one hundred percent filled with female patrons. Slowly women began to single out particular male performers who took their fancy and then return again and again *specifically* to see them. These actors became the matinee idols.

The question of whether the times make the man or vice versa is no problem in the case of Harry Montague. He came when the matinee came and was its first favorite, an example of the new power of women as an index of public taste. This is not to deny Montague's attractions. He was a suave and talented British import, highly cultured in the stage refinements and more than unusually presentable. But many other cultured Britishers had come and gone before his time and none had gained such attention. They were all denied the essential ingredient, the matinee.

Montague was discovered by Dion Boucicault, an indefatigable actor-manager of the early days of American melodrama. He spotted Montague in a cabaret in San Francisco's Bohemian Club, and was so impressed with his abilities (it must be stated that the evening Boucicault saw Montague, Montague was singing one of

Harry Montague and Ada Dyas in The Shaughraun.

Contemporary caricature of Harry Montague.

Boucicault's own songs) that he persuaded him to come east and there introduced him to Henry Wallack, owner of the famous theater that bore his name.

The atmosphere at Wallack's Theater was the perfect culturing medium for young Montague, whose Cary Grant-like sense of light comedy was brought to bloom in the high comedies performed by Wallack's company. This company not only included the great Boucicault but a wonderful player of matrons and *grandes dames* named Elizabeth Ponisi, the comedian extraordinaire, John Gilbert, and E. L. Davenport, one of the most important actors in America. Montague was introduced to New York in a play called *The Romance of a Poor Young Man* in 1874 and five years later was Wallack's greatest luminary. By now the matinee was going strong and women attended his shows by the thousands. Henry Wallack watched, no doubt in amazement, as dainty ladies shoved and not so gently shouldered for position at the ticket counters, stood in packs at the back of the theater when tickets sold out, tried to sneak in on the fire escapes when standing room was taken. Plays were interrupted by women climbing onto the stage, and sometimes a half dozen had to be escorted out of one performance. Everywhere he went droves followed, and he finally judged it expedient to hire a bodyguard to protect him from the fair sex.

William Brady, the promoter and manager, saw Montague play to these raucous crowds and leaves us with this impression: "Montague was the first matinee idol I knew in the American theater. Matinee audiences couldn't get enough of him. His mail was like a movie star's today. Hundreds of women used to collect at the stage doors every day to watch Harry come and get out of his carriage—the kind of mob adulation which has since been transferred to screen idols on an even bigger scale."

Brady makes another assertion, which may or may not be true: "The word 'matinee idol,' " he says, "the matinee being the big time for female audiences, was coined to suit his case."

For some time Montague continued to titillate congregations of worshipful fans. But at the peak of his success the congregants were astounded to find he had coughed himself to death in a San

A typical theater of the 1880's when Montague was in his prime. This playhouse, with its caryatids, fringed curtains, ornate banisters, and rococo reliefs, was obviously built to please feminine tastes. The matinee in process, perhaps Romeo and Juliet, has the accompaniment of full orchestra. The house is ninety percent filled with women.

One of the many "floral tributes" sent by Montague's fans to mourn his premature death.

Francisco hotel room as a result of a ruptured lung. The news launched a small empire of women into mourning. As in the Valentino demonstrations yet to come, they built gigantic altars of flowers with his initials spelled out in red carnations, wore black ribbons across their hearts, and paced sobbing in front of the theaters where he had played.

Actually, the whole event was something like a rehearsal for the Valentino debacle, a sensational Hollywood-style tragicomedy writ small and before its time. At Montague's funeral the crowds of lugubrious mourners who wailed for a man they had never known were smaller than the Valentino throngs, and no "woman in black" appeared. But like Valentino, it is recorded that one woman built a shrine in her closet for Harry Montague and there, at the foot of his picture, burned candles to his memory long into every night.

The Reluctant Matinee Idol

KYRLE BELLEW

"I am not a matinee idol, I never was a matinee idol, and I won't be a matinee idol," said Kyrle Bellew, the greatest matinee idol of

KYRLE BELLEW.

Playing cards with matinee idols posing between the pips were especially popular in the late nineteenth century. This deck has a different star pictured on each card.

MR. KYRLE BELLEW.

WHAT IT IS TO BE A MASHER (?)

The press was fond of lampooning matinee idols and often pictorialized them as the haughty fops we see here. In 1889, Life magazine, which was then devoted mostly to humorous articles, included Bellew in its "Gallery of Players" and caricatured the tale of his travels:

"We place little confidence in the story that he [Bellew] was kidnapped while a child of twenty-one or twenty-two by a beautiful duchess who bore him off to a tropical isle in an equatorial sea, and conferred on him the office of maid in the nursery of her grand-children, whence he escaped in the baby carriage and joined Henry Irving who was then starring in the East Indies in Uncle Tom's Cabin.

"The tale that Kyrle ran away from home at age sixteen, and took command of a Moorish pirate ship on the Mediterranean, which made a practice of stealing fruit from the coast guard steamers and eating it on a desert island, seems more plausible."

the 1880's. Like Harry Montague, Bellew was an Englishman, and like Montague, he landed, despite himself, in the middle of the matinee girl's lap. The story of his life, and it is a romantic one, was told and retold to his fans a hundred times.

He was born in India in 1857, the eldest son of the Bishop of Calcutta who, before his conversion to Catholicism, had been chaplain for Queen Victoria. Bellew went to Oxford but soon tired of the scholastic life and ran away to sea where he joined the crew of the cruiser *Conway*. At the end of his eight-year enlistment he decided to be an actor and teamed up with an ingénue named Cora Potter. They traveled to the Orient and were the first to bring Shakespeare to newly opened Japan. Then they visited the Nizam of Hyderabad in India, who sent a train of fifty elephants to receive them. They entertained the Nizam for eight hours with Shakespearean drama until it was announced that the great potentate had fallen sound asleep and no longer wished to be disturbed.

At the end of his tour Bellew returned to London, with no money and an empty stomach. He answered an ad seeking a comedian and was taken on by a rural playhouse at two pounds a week. A critic saw Bellew perform, was impressed, and wrote of him to Dion Boucicault. Boucicault, who had also discovered Harry Montague, was likewise impressed, gave Bellew a position at the Haymarket Theater in London, and there he soon became a regular.

In 1885 Bellew came to America, where he was pursued by matinee girls with such hysteria that one writer compared his popularity to a fifteenth-century dancing mania. The matinee girls, being strictly American creations, took Bellew by surprise. They learned when he took his daily walk and followed him. They

Kyrle Bellew's beloved profile in 1885 (left) and in 1902 (center). Kyrle as Romeo, Eleanor Robson as Juliet. (Right)

THE THEATRE
AN ILLUSTRATED MAGAZINE OF THEATRICAL AND MUSICAL LIFE

KYRLE BELLEW as "Romeo"

stood outside the theater in the rain, the snow, the mud, in defiance of their chaperons, just to say "I saw Bellew." They built shrines for him in their bureaus and founded fan clubs in his name, the first, incidentally, ever started for an entertainer. When he finally left America in 1888 the docks were a swirling, weeping mass of femininity, and in the papers the next day it was reported that two girls had tried to stow away on his ship and one had jumped into the water after it.

While Bellew was in America he maintained with insistence that he was *not* a matinee idol but a genuine representative of the old-school Shakespearean tradition. His overly grandiloquent Shakespearean technique, however, admired as it was by young belles, was considered even in the 1880's to be slightly "camp." Playing Romeo with chest thrust out and arms akimbo, with face to the heavens and hands to the breast, people sometimes thought he was deliberately parodying the Bard. But women didn't care. They just liked to look at him. And they liked his plays as well, saber-smashing melodramas with lots of love and plenty of gore. A favorite was *A Gentleman of France,* in which Bellew killed no less than seventeen men—four marquises, six viscounts, three servants, and four pedestrians, all slain on a cineramically longitudinal staircase in the middle of the stage. At the end of the drama the proscenium was strewn with perforated supernumeraries while our hero, unruffled in fluffy linens, patent leather boots, and red tights, ardently kissed a marchioness as the final curtain dropped.

Bellew's flight from America did not last long. After a period of time spent searching for, and finding, gold in the bush country of Australia, he returned to America a rich man and settled down to become a rather competent actor. By the beginning of the twentieth century he had even mellowed toward his idol days and defended old-style romance against the oncoming vogue for light comedy which was sweeping his style of acting into the wings.

"Is Romeo dead, is Juliet in her tomb?" asked an interviewer.

"Forsooth, what chance hath an ardent boy like Romeo in these days of telephones and telegraphs," answered Bellew. "True, I have been drawn into many affairs of a romantic nature on the stage and have sighed a thousand times in such exquisite tortures of passion as Romeo's. But I take no credit to myself for these affairs, for I was reared with the last of the great cavaliers in a period that has passed away. Cavaliers are out of fashion and, forsooth, this age has lost the habits of romance."

The French Matinee Idol

CHARLES FECHTER

Charles Fechter was one of the great romantic dramatists in France, a hero of Dumas' early thrillers and an original Armand Duval in *Camille*. When he came to America in 1870 with his no-holds-barred type of intense performing, he hastened the "melo-romantic" movement already well launched. After witnessing an experience of Fechter in tragedy or romance, they said, one returned to all other actors and found them, by contrast, cool and starchy, and many young actors incorporated his uninhibited brand of let-loose passion into their own techniques. Later, as the stage manager of the Lyceum Theater in New York, Fechter would introduce innovations in the theater which are so common today they are taken for granted. The sunken stage, ceilings on stage

Fechter as Hamlet. "No innovation in art," wrote Charles Dickens, "was ever accepted with so much favor by so many intellectual persons, pre-committed to, and preoccupied by another system, as Fechter's Hamlet."

sets, and footlights set *below* the vision of audiences were all his inventions.

Above he is shown doing his Hamlet, famous throughout Europe for one device, the wearing of a flowing golden wig. Fechter's reasoning for this stunt was airtight: Hamlet was a Dane, Danes are fair, and therefore Hamlet undoubtedly was in real life a blond.

The Matinee Idol Despite Himself

FRANK MAYO

Many matinee idols played the same roles so many times that eventually the public would let them play no other. One case was James O'Neill, father of the playwright Eugene O'Neill, who acted in *The Count of Monte Cristo* no less than 5,342 times. "I believe," he said, "that I should have lost my memory and mind altogether had I continued to keep up the strain." Another example was Frank Mayo, captured by Frank Murdock's play, *Davy Crockett.*

Davy Crockett: the setting is the midwestern frontier, the hero is Crockett, a quiet, rugged fellow, untutored in the niceties but prevailingly upright, as honest as Diogenes, and as strong as Babe the Blue Ox. The heroine, Eleanor Vaughn, is a spoiled pure-blood from the east who, despite her air of haughty assumption, is really all right down deep. They fall in love. He saves her from a snowstorm, blackmail, a lubricious villain, wolves. He instructs her in the fundamentals of life, she simplifies her ways, they live happily, etc.

For the easterner who already considered the west a symbol of escape from industrially revolutionized New York, it was the American version of the enlightened savage. The play was taken so seriously that some actually headed west because of it, and from its pages came an abundance of dramatic myths used later in many cowboy pictures: the strong, silent pioneer ranger, the easterner who finds happiness out west, the triumph of the simple

Mayo instructs his son, Edwin, in the tedious art of playing Davy Crockett.

forest dweller over the city slicker, and of course the love story of a western lad who loves and marries a haughty back-east heiress. "The element which gives *Davy Crockett* its claim to success," wrote the critic Hewitt, "is a simple story of pure love that runs through the play like a thread of gold. It is the poem of young Lochinvar dramatized and americanized."

In buckskin jacket and coonskin cap which his latter-day namesake, Fess Parker, would popularize under the Disney standard, Mayo's picture was on every woman's shelf and helped make the wearing of animal skins chic. He played the role again and again, and theatergoers never tired of watching him. Whenever he attempted a new play the icy silence that greeted him sent him back to his furs, and gradually he became ensnared in his own coonskin. As the years passed he began to hate the play and continued to hate it until he died. But even death did not bring complete escape; like the sins of the father, the role of Davy Crockett was visited on Mayo's son, Edwin, who went on to act the part so many times that he too, like his father, came to hate the play that made his fortune.

MAURICE BARRYMORE.

SOME years ago there was produced in a New York theatre a play in which Madame Modjeska acted the part of the heroine and Maurice Barrymore was the hero. On its first night a reporter on the *New York Herald* was detailed to send "notes" to his paper. When the play was over the reporter and the author of the play adjourned to a chop house and were discussing old days when they were "cramming" for Indian Civil Service at Walter Wren's in London. Maurice Barrymore dropped in and joined the party. "What, were you fellows at Wren's?" he asked. "So was I. Don't you remember Herbert Blythe?"

Of course they remembered Herbert Blythe, a sort of fleeting shadow who had the reputation of being a brilliant scholar, of knowing how to manage his "dukes" better than any amatuer boxer of his day and of never attending any class save when the late Prof. Thorold Rogers was talking scandal against Queen Elizabeth. It was a strange reunion, this meeting of three of Wren's pupils, twenty years or so after they had left Powis Square and thousands of miles away from their native heath. But pleasant as it was strange; for Maurice Barrymore is a delightful companion and has this advantage over most of his fellow players—he is educated. He was at Cambridge before he went to Wren's, and when he gave up all idea of serving the Kaiser I. Hind in India he "ate his dinners" and became a barrister. But soon got weary of Blackstone and Broome and being a born Bohemian—although his father was a clergyman of the Established Church—he drifted on to the stage. He came to this country and made his first appearance at the Fifth Avenue Theatre, New York. At once he was accepted by the public—especially the female portion of it—as one of the best of the imported *jeunes premiers* and Maurice Barrymore's photographs sold like wildfire. Splendidly built and very handsome in face, he could easily have stepped into the shoes of Harry Montague who, charming actor that he was, was never what Maurice Barrymore could have been had Barrymore so chosen. But "Barry," as his intimates who have known him since he adopted the stage as a profession call him, "Herbie," as he is called by those who knew him before, did not chose. He has rarely shown the public what his capabilities are. There is no man on the American stage to-day who can play the melodramatic hero better than he if he wants to; none his superior in refined comedy would he only give his mind to it. When one knows what a really brilliant man Maurice Barrymore is, how far ahead he is in talent of most of the successful actors on our boards, one feels inclined to kick him as he shambles through his part. The great trouble, however, about kicking him is that, in prize ring parlance, he would very soon send his kicking critic "to sleep."

Barrymore is a playwright as well as a player. His "Nadjesda," written for Madame Modjeska, is a very powerful play, but there was an incident in the plot which the public, at the time it was produced, could not digest. So it failed. The public stomach has since these days become very strong and, had we a Sarah Bernhardt to play the title part, we imagine "Nadjesda" would now draw crowded houses. He also wrote the book of "The Robber of the Rhine," which was utterly unworthy of his talents.

MAURICE BARRYMORE

Maurice Barrymore the lackadaisical, the cynical, the carelessly elegant, the keen, the perfectly bred, the forgetful, the wise, the billiard sharp, the amateur boxing champion of England, the great actor cast into the shadows by amateur lunkheads, the leading man every female star wanted as a consort not because he could act, although he sometimes could, but because he had "swagger" and taught American actors *how* to swagger and was the man of whom swagger finally came to be expected and never bothered to do anything else.

Maurice Barrymore, the society swell with the heart of gold, the good fellow with too many friends, the *jeune premier* whose picture women wore in lockets, the adventurer born in India in the British-held Red Fort in Agra while outside the walls of this ancient palace the Indian Mutiny of 1847 blazed in oriental ferocity and his mother gave birth to her son in a dungeon whose windows looked out on the Taj Mahal, pink and noble, across the Jumna River.

Maurice Barrymore, born Herbert Blythe, who took the stage name Barrymore so his very proper parents wouldn't know their son had jumped a Cambridge education to exercise his true muse in the old West End, who married Georgie Drew, and had three children with her and John Drew as a brother-in-law, who spent the last years of his life hopelessly deranged in an insane asylum on Long Island, writing an epic poem that went on forever and nobody could understand.

Maurice Barrymore the poet, Maurice Barrymore the playwright, Maurice Barrymore the debaucher, Maurice Barrymore the actor capable of fluffing every line in the play or forgetting to show up at all while the women in the balcony, two hundred strong, stamped their feet and whistled as some meek manager announced from a very small corner of the stage that Mr. Barrymore had been "detained," which he no doubt had, at the Lamb's Club, telling hilarious dirty stories or recounting how he'd come to America in

Madame Modjeska in 1884, for many years Maurice Barrymore's most popular leading lady.

'74 and played Augustin Daly's *Under the Gaslight* where he was supposed to be saved from the wheels of a railroad train but the mechanical contraption driving the damned locomotive wouldn't work and he lay there tied to the tracks calling the cue for the train six times and Augustin Daly pulled his hair and fired the cast three times, or how he wrote *Nadjeska* for that fiery Pole, Madame Modjeska, who considered herself the rival of Bernhardt, and how Modjeska cried when she read the script.

Maurice Barrymore, who went home each dawn in monocle and top hat, and sang his drunken Irish tunes so loud he woke up Lionel and Ethel and little John, whose names would be recalled long after his became a footnote or paragraph at best. Maurice Barrymore, who sometimes read himself to sleep with lines Lackaye tossed off one night and handed him across the bar and which for no damn reason in the world had bothered him ever since:

> I talked beneath the moon
> I slept beneath the sun
> I lived a life of going-to-do
> And I died with nothing done.

Although Barrymore was equally at home in a tuxedo or a suit of armor, he was essentially a modern-day hero, at his best in quickly paced contemporary dialogue dramas such as *Captain Swift,* in which he is pictured above. The following is how one

Maurice Barrymore as Captain Swift, his most famous role.

reviewer described the story of *Captain Swift:* "Maurice Barrymore as Wielding, the mysterious hero in *Captain Swift,* had been a highwayman in Australia and had come to England to live a better life among people to whom he was a stranger. Indeed? Marshall, the old butler, recognized him by the scar on his wrist. Mr. Gardner, an Australian squatter, recognized his voice as that of the highwayman who robbed him in Queensland. Henry Woodruff, jealous of his attentions to the beautiful Stella, recognized him as an adventurer. Stella, infatuated with the mysterious stranger, recognized him as the man of her dreams. Annie Russell, by instinct, recognized him as a bad man. Lady Betty Phillips recognized him as the infant she had sent out of the country to preserve her sister's reputation. Lady Betty Phillip's sister recognized him as her long-lost son. Finally, Walden Ramsay, an Australian detective, recognized him as Captain Swift and produced a warrant for his arrest."

Although Barrymore was one of the most famous actors of his era, his best-known exploit took place outside a theater. In 1878 he was in the southwest where he and his theatrical company were touring in Sardou's play, *Diplomacy.* He was fresh out of New York and like his contemporary, Harry Montague, was riding high on the new matinee craze that had just broken in the east. On this day, however, in a small Texas town where matinees were unknown and actors were the lowest caste, he was far from Broadway. After the evening's performance, accompanied by a young actress and a fellow performer named Ben Porter, Barrymore went to the local saloon for dinner. There a burly sheriff named Jim Curry was seated on a nearby stool and he, obviously sharing the local disinclination for actors, made an obscene remark to the young actress. Barrymore sprinted to defend her honor. He was once amateur boxing champion of England and was not afraid of a mix with the redoubtable sheriff. But the sheriff, who had never heard of the Marquess of Queensbury, pulled his revolver and shot Barrymore in the shoulder. Ben Porter jumped off his seat and rushed to help, and Curry fired into his face, killing him instantly.

BENJAMIN C. PORTER, *Assassinated in Marshall, Texas, March 20.*   MAURICE BARRYMORE, *Wounded in Marshall, Texas, March 20.*

Back east the news made immediate headlines, but it took more than two years before the case came to trial. When it did a jury of local rednecks found the sheriff innocent and Curry was set free. He traveled to New Orleans and there he died when an itinerant actor, whose name was never known, shot him in the face in a barroom brawl.

THE MATINEE LADIES

Madge Lessing (name of woman pictured on facing page). Since it takes two to tango, every matinee man needed a matinee lady. Without her his identity had no meaning. These ladies came in all shapes and personalities—innocent and wanton, athletic and demure, contemplative and toujours gaie—*someone for every taste. Many of them were strikingly beautiful, yet they rarely gathered enormous followings of men in the way their male counterparts collected women. Indeed, there never really was a female equivalent to the matinee idol, for aside from a few sugar daddies and assorted stage door Johnnies, men seldom came in masses specifically to see female performers. It seems, furthermore, that this fact carries over into a paradox that has long prevailed: in private relationships it is men that pursue, but when romance is writ large in mass entertainment, women become the prime aggressors. Be that as it may, during matinee season women, if not idolized in the style of men, were still the* sine qua non *of romantic theater, and as such were immensely popular. A few of them are pictured here.*

Amelia Bingham as Mother Nature

Agnes Lee

*Marie Jansen, an
extremely popular actress.*

*Louise Lester, bearing the actress's
badge of infamy, a cigarette.*

Rose Coghlan

Imogene. During the late nineteenth century it was common for an actress to be known only by her first name.

Belle Archer

Rachel Booth

CHAUNCEY OLCOTT

There were few other actors in America who had as faithful a following as Chancellor John Olcott. He was born in Buffalo, New York, and began his career in the 1880's with Emerson and Hooley's Minstrel Show.

In these days the minstrel shows were the most popular form of itinerant entertainment in the United States. They moved from town to town in dumpy railroad cars and played one-nighters in any location populated enough to have a town hall. The entire town would turn out to see them perform the inevitable black-face routines or the hootchy-kootchy dances, banjo solos, trained animal acts, fiddle and tambourine duets, or to sing such well-known favorites as "Picayune Butler," "Four Little Curly-headed Darkies," and "Oh, Tiny, Play That Traumerai."

The height of the evening came when some handsome crystal-voiced ballad singer closed the show with a soapy lullaby. Olcott was one of these singers. But in the minstrel shows one needed a gimmick to give the act some mystique. So Olcott billed himself as an Irish tenor (as far as we know, he had never been to Ireland, and there was always some question as to whether he was really Irish at all), and soon made a reputation as a popular crooner.

When he left the blackface syndrome for the stage it was only logical that he would continue his career as a professional Irishman. At this time New York City was a haven for millions of Irish emigrants who had fled the potato famines. These emigrants, living in a hostile city whose storefronts posted signs reading "No Irish need apply," sought consolation and escape from loneliness through any entertainment that reminded them of home. Many performers were quick to exploit this lucrative market, but none was more popular than W. J. Scanlon, the reigning king of the Irish-American theater. When he died in 1898 no one could fill the gap, but Scanlon's manager, Augustus Piton, hated to lose a good thing and searched relentlessly for a replacement until he discovered Olcott.

Chauncey Olcott who was, as the Latins said, "Hibernicis ipsis Hibernior"—more Irish than the Irish.

A group of nineteenth-century minstrels.

By the beginning of the twentieth century Olcott had thoroughly replaced Scanlon in the hearts of the Irish. They, however, scarcely having the money to afford a rich man's New York theater, patronized theaters of their own known as the "subway circuits"—showhalls reachable only by tram—which included off-Manhattan houses as close to Broadway as the Bushwick in Brooklyn and as far as the Shubert in Newark. In these places Olcott made his fortune. Here he played a hundred simple love

stories: boy meets girl, boy loses girl, boy gets girl, the performances interlarded with maudlin Irish tunes. "Chauncey's delight and forte," said an observer, "were in the scenes that smacked of fairy-land, glimpses of that fanciful world where all is beauty, and love is master. Many a tear was shed in his audiences, but the smiles were numerous and everyone went from them as happy as a child after a bedtime story." Always he was cast as the gallant knight, the *chevalier sans peur* about to embark on a journey of

Olcott's delight— scenes that smacked of fairyland, glimpses of that fanciful world where all is beauty and love is master.

Olcott and the children. "Men," he once said, "are only wee things grown too big to believe in elves."

adventure to the Isle of Love. Now he is a jolly rogue fighting for Ireland's freedom; now he is a Gallic prince pledged to save his betrothed from her wicked uncle; now he is the captain of the frigate *Connamora,* standing on her burning deck while below the seas are churned by six schoolboys beneath a green tarpulin, each paid five cents to make waves in the canvas by flutter kicking, while on deck the captain sings a goodbye ballad to his beloved in the far-off Emerald Isles.

If other actors hated being typecast or if they struggled to free themselves from the limiting constriction of a particular image, Olcott had no such insecurities. He was happily and forever Irish, the blarneystone Romeo. He loved everything Irish, wore a shamrock pin, dressed in green, and signed autographs "Yours in Irish." But though "serious" playgoers sneered at him and dubbed him the "Servant Girl's Caruso," Olcott nevertheless made real contributions to the American repertoire of songs. "My Wild Irish Rose," "Mother Machree," and most famous of all, "When Irish Eyes are Smiling," were all tunes he wrote and sang again and again, and again once more for the Irish audiences that adored him.

The Funny Matinee Idol

HENRY DIXEY

Here is Henry Dixey playing Adonis in *Adonis*. If he looks ridiculous he was meant to—at least sort of. The play was about a beautiful marble statue of Adonis, played by Mr. Dixey, that was suddenly brought to life, turned into the twinkle-toed godling pictured here, and pursued across a stageland Arcadia by a bevy of beautiful Olympian sylphs. The whole thing was interspersed with Mr. Dixey's dance numbers, animal imitations, and stand-up gags. Starting out as a parody of stage romances, *Adonis* opened at Hooley's theater in Chicago on July 6, 1884, and ended up making Dixey into the love god he lampooned. His piles of "mash" letters from girls all over America and England became so vast they were

Henry Dixey as Adonis (left). Dixey was not the only actor to spoof the matinee idol. This assortment of droll-looking gentlemen was the whimsical product of romantic satires.

said to exceed even Lillian Russell's collection (women got them too), and from his lowly beginnings playing the forelegs in a cow costume as a replacement for some other actor who had inadvertently kicked the manager across the stage Dixey became almost everybody's darling. His arrivals and departures were noted with the greatest concern; his opinions on every subject were solicited, from presidential elections to fashions in women's umbrellas; the novelist William Dean Howells (*The Rise of Silas Lapham*) recruited him to write articles for his literary magazine on subjects he knew nothing about; he was entertained by the prime minister of England; and when *Adonis* passed its five hundredth performance, it was celebrated by a ball at the Metropolitan Opera House in New York City. Dixey went on to do Adonis over a thousand times, a record for the number of performances given in one play. How appropriate that the matinee idol establishing such an impressive figure should do it in the role of the love god.

The Horrifying Matinee Idol

WILTON LACKAYE

For a generation Wilton Lackaye strutted and fretted through countless dramas. He played Nero with a stageful of lions. He played the general in *Shenandoah*. He played the private in *The Frisky Mrs. Johnson*. He was an old man in *The Battle*. He was a young man in *Money Mad*. He was at one time or another the hero, the heavy, the eccentric, the madman, the doctor, the comedian, the monster, the fop, the adolescent, the lawyer, the drawing room gentleman, the servant, the soldier, the priest, the cavalier, and practically every other stock character ever to walk out of a melodrama. Like other turn-of-the-century workhorse performers, he might be called to play any of these roles at a moment's notice, and it is not difficult to understand why such actors occasionally got their plays confused and delivered the third act of *Bertha the Sewing Machine Girl* in the first act of *King Lear*.

Then in 1894 it was announced that George du Maurier's book, *Trilby*, would be dramatized. Considered a great work of

Wilton Lackaye, a nineteenth-century workhorse performer.

art in its time, today *Trilby* is deemed a minor literary curiosity. But though the book is almost forgotten, its most interesting character, Svengali, lives on, king of the mountebanks, hypnotist par excellence, and seducer of helpless victims, female variety, through the Mephistophelian force of his animal magnetism.

The play opened in 1895 with Lackaye in the role of Svengali, and immediately a curious phenomenon was noted at the box office: more ladies were coming to see this play than had come to the theater in years. Attendance had not been good of late. The novelty of the matinee had by this time worn off a bit, and whereas afternoon performances in the 1880's had without fail played to capacity houses, the next decade saw a brief decline in female attendance. All the more amazing, then, that women crammed the theaters for matinees of *Trilby*. What was the reason? Did women see themselves in the role of the helpless Trilby, overcome by the provocative forces of darkness? Perhaps. But who was the protagonist of this darkness if not Svengali himself? Yes, it was certain. Despite his John L. Lewis eyebrows, his brute, bulbous eyes and matted beard, and despite, or perhaps because of, the merciless manner by which he rendered women helpless to his will, Svengali was the silver hook of the play.

Historically, matinee idol villains were not new with Svengali. It had always been known that the appeal of the diabolical, provided it was embodied by a good stock of male charisma, brought women to the playhouse. Nor was it a coincidence that so many of these bad guys were also not so bad looking. To watch the heroine pursued by some Quasimodo was dreary for female audiences; but to see her threatened by a Desperate Desmond almost as attractive as the hero himself was another story entirely. So for years women watched in secret admiration as these caped, dark-mustached heels seductively tried to destroy the hopes and sometimes even the chastity of the female lead.

But Svengali was different. He wasn't handsome, he was ugly. He *was* Quasimodo. He was, in fact, totally disgusting, as his picture here attests. He was everything a Victorian lady fainted over and professed to despise, and yet . . .

Human psychology is a most curious thing. The ladies flocked to see Svengali, and he became the villain above all others whom the women, hypnotized along with Trilby, most deliciously hated themselves for loving.

The stage villain. "Be cruel, but elegant," instructed Lowell Sherman, a stage and film idol famous for his skilled villainy. "Lift your eyebrow thus—while you lift the club. After you have betrayed them, meet their reproaches with an icy, inscrutable, irritating smile. When you have them in your power, which takes about five minutes, hurt their feelings continuously but sauvely, delicately, elegantly. Scrutinize them through your monocle, then tell them they are not looking well. But smile."

Wilton Lackaye as Svengali.

A handful of hard-core villains at work.   One tries to punch the heroine in the stomach, another, looking like a young Robert Morley, watches in amusement, while a third picks his teeth revoltingly as he looks lewdly at the hapless lady. Fortunately for virtue's sake, two stouthearted heroes are present to restrain the scoundrels.

The Athlete-Turned-Matinee Idol

JAMES J. CORBETT

In the 1890's prizefighters were not strangers to the stage. John L. Sullivan had played in *Honest Hearts and Willing Hands* (the title fully characterizes the play), and Bob Fitzsimmons, shirtless, hammered out real horseshoes on a real forge in *The Honest Blacksmith*. But neither of these men was especially handsome.

Then in 1892 James J. Corbett knocked out John L. Sullivan

for the world's championship, and James J. Corbett *was* handsome. Wherever he fought, ladies put on ties and jackets and sneaked into the all-male boxing arenas to see him at fisticuffs. Corbett's manager quickly recognized his faculties of allurement and exploited them. He filmed Corbett's fights and turned them into the first commercial sportsreels ever made. He exhibited him at the Folies-Bergère where, he tells us, *ah qu'il est beau,* said the ladies of the cabaret. He charged women extravagant admissions to watch Corbett skip ropes and punch bags, and eventually he pocketed thousands by marketing plaster-cast paperweights of Jim's tapered fist.

Then one day Corbett decided he would become an actor. He made his debut in Dion Boucicault's melodrama *After Dark,* a play still remembered for introducing the motif of the hero tied to the railroad tracks, and the critics gave him tolerable notices. Next he toured England in a play written for him called *Gentleman Jim,* and thus typecast as none other than himself, he was a smash success. Finally he became somewhat too ambitious. "I wish to do serious acting," he said, and opened in Bernard Shaw's play *Cashel Byron's Profession.* The critics broiled him. "Ex-champ Corbett had a mill with Bernard Shaw last night," wrote one of them, "and knocked him out in three rounds."

Wrote William Brady: "The female of the species raised more sand over James Corbett than over any matinee idol in the business." Here is Corbett looking amazingly intact considering he often went sixty rounds with bare fists. "Nobody ever put a mark on Jim Corbett," said Brady. "After a long ring career his Roman nose was just as shapely as ever."

ROBERT MANTELL

Fanny Davenport

Robert Mantell

In 1883 New York playgoers anxiously await the opening of Sardou's new play, *Fedora*. Sardou is everybody's favorite playwright, and excitement runs high about his new production. The play will star Fanny Davenport, daughter of the famous actor, E. L. Davenport, and also promises to advance some exciting new talents, among them a Scotsman named Robert Bruce Mantell. Already Fanny Davenport has spent thirty-five thousand dollars of her own savings on the production, most of which is engineered to make certain that the lighting, direction, costumes, and makeup will do everything possible to hold her in the spotlight, for an opening in New York is an important event for any performer, even one as established as Fanny Davenport.

On first night the theater is filled with New York celebrities, joined by the social and intellectual elite—the writers, actors, critics, and intelligensia that are making New York the most important city in nineteenth-century America. As the curtain goes up all eyes are in the direction of Miss Davenport. She receives a warm ovation, but it is soon apparent that the house is cold and reserved. They applaud the supporting cast with mechanical politeness that damns with faint praise, and though Miss Davenport receives her due, there will quite definitely be no trimmings. By the end of the second act she is almost in tears, for her grand opening is decidedly laying an egg. Mantell has received his share of courteous disregard with the rest. He finds Miss Davenport backstage. "We'll hit 'em next time, the icebergs," he promises, but she scarcely hears him.

The third act begins and the drama builds. The audience becomes alert.

Fedora, played by Miss Davenport, confronts Louis Ipanoff, played by Mantell. Her lover has been murdered and she suspects that Louis has done it. She questions him again and again in a dialogue of increasing intensity. He will admit nothing.

Up to this point Mantell has played his part with subdued composure, keeping appropriately out of Miss Davenport's way;

but now something takes him over and he can scarcely control his own commanding magnitude.

Murmurs of excitement are heard in the audience as he displays a mounting fury over Fedora's cross-examination. Fedora cajoles him, pleads with him, screams at him, then accuses him directly of the murder, but he denies the crime. Fedora throws herself at his feet and the scene builds to a point of almost unbearable tension. Finally he snaps.

Yes, yes, yes, he has killed Fedora's lover. Had he not found this man and his own lover together, she in his arms, he making love to her in unabashed passion? Yes, he has done it, and he regrets nothing, nothing!

The audience is now completely taken with the electric force of Mantell. Someone almost falls out of the balcony. Two people in the front row stand up and shout, totally absorbed in the flow of the exchange.

"Kill him!" screams Fedora, and members of the audience shout back, "Yes, kill him, kill the scoundrel!"

Mantell in turn thunders back an even louder volley of such

In local town halls such as this, Mantell and other itinerant troopers made the best of hick audiences, dowdy costumes and cramped prosceniums to bring Shakespeare before the American hinterlands. Here The Merchant of Venice *is being performed. Note the musicians in the pit —Shakespeare was often presented with orchestral accompaniment.*

Robert Mantell toward the end of his career, an aging Romeo.

force that Miss Davenport later admitted she was frankly intimidated by the man's crushing delivery. Mantell fills the theaters with his presence. By the end of the scene the entire audience is on its feet, shouting bravos, swinging their arms wildly, applauding in thunderous accord, and the name they call is Mantell's.

For almost fifty years after this night Robert Mantell remained a favorite god of the gallery. He signed with the producer Daniel Frohman at ten thousand dollars a year and proceeded to fill the theater with women who watched him grind his teeth, wring his hands, tear his hair, stamp his feet, roll his eyes, and pound his breast, always in the service of love. One day, in the midst of these histrionics, a warrant was issued for his arrest. He had neglected to pay alimony to his first wife (he would have four of them), and he fled from New York.

By covered wagon, iron horse, horseback, muleback, camelback, he toured the United States in exile. One of the last blood-and-thunder Shakespeareans, Mantell brought *Macbeth* to a hundred one-horse towns across the country that otherwise might never have heard of the Bard. Later he received a reprieve, returned to New York to do Shakespeare, then some vaudeville, and finally in 1915 a short career in the photoplays.

But like an ordinary mortal touched but once by the finger of the gods, never again was Robert Mantell able to perform with such surpassing brilliance as the night he became a star in *Fedora*.

The Drawing Room Matinee Idol

JOHN DREW

In March of 1875 word was out that the famous manager, Augustin Daly, was having trouble with his leading man, George Clark. Daly was something of a martinet during rehearsals, and one of his eccentricities was that he forbade his actors to wear mustaches during the performance of Sheridan plays. Clark owned a fine handlebar and was loath to shave it, a fight ensued, and Daly was soon short one leading man. He remembered a young actor he had seen in Philadelphia, a man named John Drew, and wrote for his services. Drew arrived, *sans* mustache. He was given a role in *The Big Bonanza*, a wish-fulfillment comedy about getting rich quick on the stock market, and was soon Daly's new leading man.

For years Drew perambulated graciously through over thirty of Daley's finest productions as the devil-may-care, slightly bored dandy who beneath an aloof façade possessed an Apollonian heart. He teamed up with the actress Ada Rehan, who became his favorite stage inamorata for years. "Beautiful, like a Romney or Gainsborough, supple, opulent, bewitching," was how she was described by the critic William Winter. Together they personified the *dernier cri* in light romance, a genre which the British polished to a shiny point of excellence and which was thought to be beyond the ca-

John Drew, head in hands, in the play Butterflies. *"She's above you, just as my love is above me," exclaims the gentleman on Drew's right. But Drew is not happy. "Why, why?" he cries. (Right) John Drew and his Irish leading lady, Ada Rehan.*

*In imitation of such love teams as Drew-Rehan and the Castles (left)
were couples who specialized in spoofing the eternal romantic. Fred
Soloman and Sylvia Gerish (middle). The Midgleys (right).*

pacities of their unsophisticated cousins across the sea. Enter Mr.
Drew to set things right. Here was the American Englishman, Sir
Osbert Pettyforth himself in Yankee flesh, our own version of the
beau monde portrayed each matinee for all to witness and con-
gratulate themselves upon: we were civilized after all—just look
at Mr. Drew.

It was the era of the Vanderbilts and the Fricks, when railroad barons were importing European châteaus stone by stone and
gentlemen really did dress for dinner in tails. This moneyed no-
bility was a thriving concern by the 1880's, and accordingly polite
drawing room drama became popular as never before. John Drew,
in tailor-made tuxedo, trim black mustache, and slicked-down black
hair, was a wealthy mother's dream escort for her debutante daughter, the ideal drawing room Lothario, and he became a favorite *bon
ton* actor. Nor were the types that he played total fictions. They
were idealized versions of the society man, no doubt, perhaps sometimes even the servant girl's version, but they nevertheless represented a type that once existed, an aristocrat with sensibilities
exclusively indigenous to American breeding, a type that all but
disappeared by the middle of the twentieth century. Playing such
roles, Drew and others like him made it legit for an American to
act English, made it OK and even sexy for native actors to be fancy-
pants and put on airs. Previously this was the visiting Englishman's
prerogative. Now it was Mr. Drew's.

Mr. Drew in courtly costume, with friend (left). Although his early career was spent as a woman's favorite, Drew, like many other matinee idols, later became an excellent actor and by the time he died was known as "the first gentleman of the American stage." Charles Coghlan (center), Herbert Kelcey (right), both forerunners of the Drew tradition. Coghlan, who had understudied Harry Montague in England, came to America in 1876, where his cool, unemotional delivery was a relief from the florid effusiveness of many American performers. In the States he and his sister, Rose Coghlan, pictured above with the matinee ladies, were instrumental in popularizing British-American swank. Herbert Kelcey was also an Englishman who quickly discovered that the U.S.A. was a paradise for good-looking young actors. He came here in 1882 and soon became more American than Abner Doubleday, who, incidentally, he resembled. Called a "glass of fashion," he obliged those who nominated him for the best-dressed man in New York City by letting it be known that he changed his clothes seven times a day and owned three hundred jackets. Because he wore kid gloves and patent leathers and played the polished Romeo in so many society plays, a critic called him "a gallant heart pumping blood too blue to stain a black tuxedo."

If Drew's style was a bit postured—one critic claimed that he rolled his eyes as if he had been playing understudy to a codfish in the last agonies of death—it was just this elegantly exasperated eye-rolling that became for thousands a trademark of all that was refined, urbane, and if a bit peevish, fashionably polite. He created a type, the tuxedoed paramour, that would influence hundreds of thoroughbreds who followed, from Ronald Colman to David Niven. "Mr. Drew is not just an elegant romantic actor," said one writer. "He is elegant romance itself."

JAMES K. HACKETT

The great matinee idol, E. H. Sothern, shown here courting Belle Archer. Sothern started his career in idoldom, graduated to serious drama, and finished as one of the most brilliant Shakespearean actors of the time.

James K. Hackett had the theater in his blood, for his father, James H. Hackett, was the greatest Falstaff ever seen on an American stage. So when James K. was sent for a gentleman's education to New York University he cut class and crossed the street to the old Lyceum Theater, where he joined other stage-struck students in the fifty-cent galleries. There he was infatuated with one star, the great matinee idol E. H. Sothern. Sothern was especially popular in swashbuckling adventures at this time in his career, and made the role of Rudolph in *The Prisoner of Zenda* famous. One day after attending a performance of this play, Hackett went backstage and questioned Sothern about becoming a successful actor. The great man was noncommittal. "Learn how to duel" was all he would say.

To understand this advice one must realize that the sword-fighting knight was the *prima persona* in the repertoire of many matinee idols. It's true that idols had to play a wide range of parts and that these parts became a round of endlessly interchanging characterizations; but from the diverse variations on the melodramatic theme the swordfighting thriller somehow stood out above all the rest in importance.

So in the later nineteenth century a primary qualification for matinee stardom was swordfighting ability. A melodrama was incomplete without a climactic duel between hero and villain. As a rule these duels were fought for the honor or protection of a woman, so naturally while the *affaire d'honneur* blazed on stage, women in the audience sat transfixed, each identifying with her sister in peril on the stage, each applauding with all her heart the brave man who was there to protect her. The more a woman attended these melodramas the more she became conditioned to believing in them, to feeling that it was really *she* whom the hero was struggling to defend. These afternoon heroes and their battles became extremely real for thousands of women (as afternoon characters in

The swordplay scene from The Prisoner of Zenda. *Hackett, the attacker, is on the right. At the end of his career Hackett allowed Adolph Zucker to film* Zenda, *although he was always so embarrassed at having appeared in it, a lowly photoplay, that he withheld the fact from* Who's Who. *All prints of the movie were destroyed in a fire not long after its production.*

television soap operas are real for millions of housewives today), and realizing that the more convincing their swordsmanship became the greater was their guarantee of capturing this female patronage, most actors took their stage fights seriously and considered them a kind of art.

A few performers neglected authenticity completely and clanked swords disinterestedly, waiting an apropriate amount of time until one of them suddenly fell dead for no apparent reason other than ennui. These were hooted off the stage by irate females who felt cheated out of a fundamental dramatic pleasure. But most were conscientious about their battles. Discussions ensued among matinee men on fine points of the duel, on details of the attack, on whether a duel was most appreciated by an audience when moving across stage or up and down. Especially debated were the alternate methods of consummating the kill. Some insisted that the most effective technique was to execute the death blow when the victim's back was to the audience, allowing the slain man to quickly grab the sword, hold it to his stomach, and spin in agonized contortions as he died. Others preferred the more difficult but highly convincing kill delivered by neatly passing

Crossed swords at the Grand Duke's Opera House in New York City. The crowd, however, appears to be all men.

"I Don't Really Kiss 'Em; I Never Have," JAS. K. HACKETT CONFESSES

"I SLIP MY THUMB ON TOP"

Famous Caress Is Phony and Leading Woman Never Gets Even a Soulful Glance

Hackett, out of cavalier's uniform for an old-fashioned parlor romance.

the blade between the victim's arm and shoulder as he stood sideways to the spectators.

Ordinarily actors fought these contests without any protection, using swords that were blunted but perfectly capable of inflicting severe injury, and there was more than one case of an actor who was actually killed in an on-stage duel. Consequently the fights were rehearsed for weeks in advance, with every thrust and parry staged for its ultimate effect; for, as every actor knew, even the worst melodrama could somehow be rescued if it finished with a roaring good fight.

And so James K. Hackett learned to duel. He studied fencing with the French master Louis Serai, and soon became amateur dueling champion of Philadelphia. His professional career had already started in this same city at the Park Theater in 1892 when he played in *The Broken Seal*, but he was still unknown outside the Quaker City. Then came the day E. H. Sothern came to town in a revival of *The Prisoner of Zenda*, and Hackett, after some manipulations, was taken on as his understudy. When Sothern left the show, Hackett replaced him as Rudolph, and so magnificently did he duel, leaping off seven-foot platforms and laughing as he tossed his sword into the air and caught it again before his assailent was upon him, that he soon overshadowed Sothern in the part. Hackett brought the show to New York. He was twenty-four, and within a year was the youngest star in the city. He then became his own manager, bought a railroad train, as actors did in those days, and toured the country with *The Prisoner of Zenda,* accompanied as he always was by his mother whom he dubbed his "matinee advisor."

For many years Hackett maintained his merry courtier image, playing adventure dramas and period pieces which inevitably cast him sword-in-hand. As a model of the knightly type, picture post-cards of him were thought wholesome enough to hang in class-rooms and Sunday schools. He modeled for them in a dozen stances, showing off his chesty physique or striking an acrobatic pose. One of these "picture pennies" that has come down to us shows him in dueling costume, his legs wrapped in sky-blue tights; and this is how he is remembered by those who saw him perform—in full cavalier's dress, standing in a jaunty posture of royal ease, roguishly pointing his foil at the moon and challenging it to a duel.

The Gentle Matinee Idol

The man who seems to be doing something slightly naughty here is Henry Miller. Actually he is only helping the young lady off with her coat (although one would never know it from the expression on her face) in the play that made him famous, *Shenandoah.* Miller was one of the stars in the stable of the producer Charles Frohman. He was discovered by Frohman in a stock company in San Francisco and there Frohman promised to hire him on the first appropriate occasion. When that occasion came, so one version of the story goes, Frohman drew a picture of himself pointing at the moon and saying "I'll make a star out of you yet," and sent it to Miller, along with a letter inviting him to join the company of *Shenandoah.* Miller accepted and for the next ten years of his forty-six in show business was one of the most popular matinee performers in the country. Neither a cape-and-sword nor a drawing room specialist, Miller was something in between, a serious and versatile player who relied on gentleness rather than physical tricks

Henry Miller   *William Faversham*

to make his romantic statement, and who never allowed himself to be identified with one play. The theater that bears his name in New York was built by him in 1918 after he turned manager, and it is today still the scene of Saturday matinees.

The Decline of the Matinee Idol

WILLIAM FAVERSHAM

When a fashion in the arts declines, the last exponents of that fashion are sometimes caricatures of the first. By the year 1910 this had happened in the world of matinee idoldom which, for all its trumpery and balderdash, had for five decades nobly entertained a nation and produced many fine actors as well. Veteran playgoers saw the once-great amorous tradition diluted with featherweight Don Juans. They saw the great matinee men pass away and waited in vain for others to take their place. They saw the melodramatic form lose its guts, grow trite and crusty and downright ridiculous, saw it transformed from the meaty thrillers of the 80's into out-and-out yellow journalism. They watched an actor like William Faversham, then in his heyday, stride stiffly upstage and proclaim his desire in a monotone voice that was amorous without ardor and sensuous without sentiment, a pathetic shadow of the romantic dramatists who had raised the hair on the heads of early nineteenth-century playwatchers and a corny imitation of those suave and competent matinee players who had ruled in the 1880's and 1890's. And as Faversham and others like him failed to keep pace with the intoxicating theatrics of the past, their vehicles also declined beneath them in rapid disintegration—for when the matinee idol died the melodrama died with him.

William Faversham was a discovery of the great star-maker Charles Frohman. Frohman found Faversham in 1887 when he

By 1900, magazines were serializing plays, using photographs from the production to illustrate the action. Here Faversham appears in one such tale. Picture stories like this became even more popular in the days of early films and helped make magazines like Photoplay *into major influences in American culture.*

Faversham as Romeo,
Maude Adams as Juliet.

was still a teenager. Faversham had been stranded in America when the British stage company he came with went bankrupt, and Frohman found him hanging around the backstage doors. Frohman put him into his latest show, an adaptation of H. Rider Haggard's novel, *She*. Even from behind a palm tree women noticed Faversham, as Frohman knew they would, and fifteen years later he was atop the romantic heap.

Tall, thin, manicured, and basically untalented, Faversham was kept a veritable prisoner for years by his female patrons who disallowed him, by force of their box office vetos, to portray any but the paramour. Before he died in 1940 he would play so many afternoon performances that his record would never be equaled and he would be remembered as "The Hero of a Thousand Matinees."

Like other stars, Faversham participated in the rituals and routines expected of an idol. He took morning constitutionals on horseback through Central Park while crowds of watchers lined the bridle paths, wore white gloves and a top hat, married enough times to satisfy the expected quota, and purchased a Long Island mansion where he raised dogs and horses (matinee idols traditionally lived on Long Island estates, perhaps because they symbolized the gentility such men reputedly possessed). But all the while he insisted, as few of the old troupers had ever done, that he didn't like acting, thought it a bore, and wished he'd stayed a plumber's assistant when, at any rate, he'd been able to sleep at night.

When matinee idols said such things audiences should have known the end was near. For a while longer people came to see Faversham and other idols, but then, from 1910 to 1915, attendance in the theaters began to drop. By 1920 it had practically reduced itself by half, and by 1930 the matinee idol was dead. The lack of talented actors, the collapse of melodrama, a shift in taste from heavy romance to light comedy, dialogue dramas and musicals, new techniques in acting which outmoded the idol's appeal— all had something to do with the idol's demise. But only something. It was not that women tired of the matinee idol. To the contrary, by 1925 they were more infatuated with him than at any other time in history. It was that the setting in which they watched him had changed; for women had deserted the playhouse with its deep pile carpets and sculptured colonnades and had gone elsewhere to look at men. Where had they gone? They had gone to the movies.

PART TWO

FILM

The First Matinee Idol of Film

FRANCIS X. BUSHMAN

In the early days of motion pictures, when film studios were known as "camps" and the word movies still had quotes around it, when critics sometimes spoke of "acts" in a film and Cecil B. De Mille rode to work through the gulches of Hollywood on a horse, Francis X. Bushman became the first major matinee idol of the cinema.

His success was due in part to a novelist and war correspondent named Richard Harding Davis, who in 1897 introduced into his novel *Soldier of Fortune* a new male prototype, a rugged but stylish hero with a muscular tapered torso, chiseled chin and aquiline profile, hair parted neatly and sideburns and beard cleanly shaved, a clean-cut, muscle-bound aristocrat, a modern American Greek god. Five years later an artist named Charles Dana Gibson, a close friend of Davis who once used the handsome writer as a model, drew this heroic specimen and called him the Gibson man. The Gibson man, like his even more famous counterpart, the Gibson girl was soon the rage of America. He became the dream image of turn-of-the-century American manhood. He set fashions in tailoring and hats, in hair style and demeanor; his profile appeared in Coca Cola ads, adorned the cover of *Collier's Weekly* magazine, was sketched in daily newspaper serials, in dime novel illustrations, everywhere; and by 1910 the Gibson man was also in the films.

Herbert Pollard, who was the original model for the Gibson man and whose face appeared in 721 places in one year, was the first of this type to enter films. He was beginning to attract attention when another actor named Francis X. Bushman arrived looking so much like a combination of Davis and Gibson's hero that Pollard was soon forgotten.

Francis X. Bushman and a Gibson-type male—jutting chin and chiseled nose.

In 1916 F.X.B. (Francis X. Bushman) and B.B. (Beverly Bayne) were the best-known initials in America. In Bushman's seven-year reign as King Romeo from 1912 to 1918, during which time sixteen secretaries were employed full-time to answer his fan mail, he made more than six million tax-free dollars, and spent it all by 1930. Courtesy, Andrew Nevai Collection

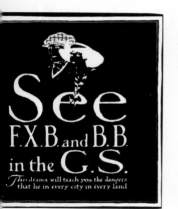

No one was quite certain what Bushman had done before he came to Hollywood. Publicity releases claimed he had held thirty-seven jobs, said he had been an acrobat, the driver of a meat wagon, a weightlifter, a professional bicyclist; even Bushman at times admitted perplexity over the motley images minted in the promotion press. Actually he was born in Baltimore in 1883 and began his show business career in 1907 in a play called *Queen of the Moulin Rouge.* Theater paid poorly if one didn't have billing, so he supplemented his income as an artist's figure model, posing at one time for the Soldiers' and Sailors' Monument in Baltimore. By 1911 photographs of him in various seminude poses had managed to catch the attention of film scouts, and he was given a contract by the Essanay Film Company, located, like so many of its competitors, in New Jersey.

"Moviestaritis" was already raging by 1910, but when Bushman went west with Essanay and started mass producing his nickelodeon specials, he carried the affliction to the American maiden community at large. The long lines of damsels that had hugged the play-houses vanished, only to reassemble in the dark passageways of the photoplay palace, where they said "oh" and "ah," not by the hundreds, nor by the thousands, nor even by the millions, but by the tens of millions, all over this one man, over this Bushman.

No saint, maharaja, pope, president, or any other single being had ever been seen or admired by so many people. Certainly no stage actor ever had, simply because he was limited by time and space—one moment, one theater, one man. Arrive Mr. Edison of New Jersey. With his coming, reality could duplicate and multiply into endless replicas of itself on celluloid. There could be one Mr. Bushman or a thousand Mr. Bushmans or a billion Mr. Bushmans, all at once, whatever you wanted. How could the legitimate theater, with its limited reproductive facilities, contend with such black magic? It couldn't, and by 1915 Bushman, with J. Warren Kerrigan, King Baggot, and Crane Wilbur & Company, had all but exterminated the matinee idol from the stage.

Francis X. Bushman and Beverly Bayne. In both photographs our idol strikes a pose which shows why he was called a "chin actor." Years later, while viewing one of his early films, Bushman remarked, "When my face flashed on that screen I laughed so hard I cried. I said 'Look at that. I'm putting all my emotions into my jaw.'"

How I Keep My Strength

By Francis X. Bushman

EDITOR'S NOTE: The leading actor of the Essanay Film Company is probably the most perfect physical specimen among the many notable athletes of the studios. His is not merely the perfection of appearance, but a reality of hard practice. He is a champion wrestler, a distance runner, a good shot, a fine rider, and a terribly dangerous antagonist in physical encounter—although, like most masters of men, Mr. Bushman is noted for his gentility and good nature.

A GREAT many people have asked me if I keep up my athletic work because I am "proud of my shape," or because it is a fad with me. To answer either question in the affirmative would be absurd. I have no pride of appearance other than that look which implies a normal and healthy human being, and a physique which serves; and while I have fads and hobbies, keeping in physical trim is not one of them. It is just as much a part of my life as eating and sleeping.

In many ways, the ancient Greeks are my ideal of a people.

Greek beauty, philosophy, architecture, bodily strength and learning have stood the test of centuries, and we, today, are not their equals in the arts or even in government. Yet the greatest thing they gave to mankind was the art of living.

Their theory can be summed up in an old proverb. I don't know who was the author of it. I wouldn't pretend to say: "The body is the urn in which the spirit burns; a spark of divine and eternal fire."

That is it: the urn of the soul and the mind. I worked on that theory. I know it is tenable. It has brought me results. Keep the body up to standard, and the mind is at its best. Let the body grow overfat, or sluggish in its functions, and the mental processes get slower.

I learned this years ago. I was given a good body to begin with, but I realized that with the passing of the first flush of youth the body would broaden, the muscles grow soft, and limbs and trunk would settle into the maturity of late adolescence. I prepared against this. I worked hard, all the time. I kept right at it, exercised not strenuously, but regularly and scientifically, and still do it, and expect to do it as long as I live. My mind is clear. I grasp every one of my play characters the better for this exercise. It is, you see, the application of the old Greek idea. The soul is contained in the body. Keep the urn bright and clean and the divine fire of the mind and soul glows more strongly.

I want to call the reader's attention to the fact which every athlete knows: that over-exercise is worse than no exercise; that sudden hard exercise is positively dangerous, and that irregular exercise is worthless.

You have probably not escaped the lazy man's wise saw: "The athlete dies young, with worn-out organs or an enlarged heart." And that

"The soul is contained in the urn of the body. Keep the urn bright and clean and the divine fire of the spirit burns more strongly."

For now he belonged to the screen, and his most superb incarnation was Francis X. Between 1911 and 1918 millions of moviegoers paid their dimes to watch "F.X.B." woo the likes of Ruth Stonehouse, Marguerite Snow, and Beverly Bayne. Especially Miss Bayne did he woo, and they became the first great romantic team in films. Bushman at the same time became the first great off-screen exhibitionist. He gave hundred-dollar tips to busboys and ordered lavender cigarettes to match his lavender boudoir and his lavender Rolls Royce. In the middle of the Essanay Studios, on his special rubber mat, he held public wrestling matches, and beefcake photos of him in a loincloth, ballooning his muscles in what looks today like a dynamic tension ad for Charles Atlas, sold like Moxie across the country. The press loved to play up this physical material, and they did, sometimes to ridiculous extremes. One article claimed that for *A Romance of the Dells* Bushman made a fifteen-foot standing leap across a chasm, a world's record, and another had it that in a sparring match with Jim Jeffries he became so excited he floored the ex-champion of the world with an angry uppercut. Nor did public relations forget to tell what a well-rounded chap he was, what his hobbies were, how he liked his steak seasoned, and how he was "the brainiest man yet produced by this new and wonderful art of films." "His," said Arthur Brisbane, the Hearst journalist, "is the best-known name and face in the world." Then in 1918 Bushman made a fatal error.

He had fallen in love with Beverly Bayne. He filed for divorce from his wife, and word got out that he was not only married but the father of five children, two facts long concealed from the public by a clause in his contract. The situation was exacerbated when lurid accounts of the divorce trial were published in the papers, and women read with horror that Mr. Bushman had beaten Mrs. Bushman and all the little Bushmans too. "Super-idol of the screen married—five children—brutal to wife," shouted the headlines in the Washington *Times* on February 10, 1918. "Fake," cried Bushman, but soon the Alhambra and Mall theaters announced they would no longer run Bushman-Bayne pictures, and across the country his votaries deserted him, forcing him into retirement.

In 1926, after eight years away from the screen, Bushman returned to play the infamous Messala and ride against Ramon Novarro in the chariot race in *Ben Hur*. He was superb in the role, too superb in fact, for when boss Louis B. Mayer caught him up-

• 89

A bit of the Bushman philosophy.

"The most handsome man in the world," in his last years.

Ramon Novarro (right) and Bushman in the famous chariot race from Ben Hur. **Courtesy, M.G.M. Studios**

staging Novarro, who was being prepped for greatness, Mayer grew irate and refused to employ Bushman in another film.

Now he began playing bit and character parts for anyone who would have him. The depression came and went with the remainder of his fortune, and he publicly offered to marry any woman who would support him. No one volunteered. So he continued to play minor parts, eventually setting a show business record by appearing in no less than twenty-five hundred roles on radio and in film. In his later years he opened an antique shop in the heart of the peepshow district on Santa Monica Boulevard in Hollywood and there, in a small house set off the street he sat among his curios looking very much like an elderly Franklin D. Roosevelt, delighted to reminisce with those who recognized him. There weren't many, the shop soon failed, and Bushman finished his career on television (he was once a villain in a *Batman* episode) as master of ceremonies on a late-night movie.

In 1966, at eighty-three, on the fortieth anniversary of the death of Valentino, the old man lost his balance while standing on a stool, hit his head on the edge of a cupboard, and died soon after. In a memorial to him, Charlton Heston, the president of the Screen Actors' Guild, said that "his passing marks the fall of one of the landmarks of Hollywood history." A short time previously Heston had been asked why he was chosen to play Ben Hur in the modern remake of the film. "There were only two of us in Hollywood who could drive a chariot," said Heston. "Francis X. Bushman is the other man, and he's too old."

LOU TELLEGEN

Lou Tellegen's reputation was based on his ability as a lover, which in turn was based on his own braggadocio. In his autobiography, *Women Have Been Kind,* he sold the public one of the most improbable lines ever manufactured by a cinematic celebrity. What is interesting is that in these pre-fan magazine days the public was so eager to believe anything they were told about stars that Tellegen's tales were readily accepted. At the same time the pipe-dreams he spun so coincided with the fantasies of his contemporaries that middle-aged adults as well as young girls patronized his films and considered him the zenith of worldly experience. With such gullibility it is no wonder that the American public provided fertile soil for the growth of film world make-believe.

Tellegen, who was a European by birth, sensed this gullibility and exploited it. He began his autobiography with an immediate far-fetched seduction scene, the first of a hundred. At fifteen, he tells us, he ran away from Russia with his father's mistress and quickly ended up in a St. Petersberg jail for selling obscene books.

A few cells down from him was a lovely female inmate who responded to his flirtatious glances, and when their respective terms expired they joined company outside the walls. The girl, it seems, was a spy and was forced to travel disguised as a Russian soldier. But the ruse failed—she was apprehended in Warsaw and sent to Siberia for life.

Tellegen moved on through central Europe and ended up at the Baron von———'s castle on the Rhine where five-day orgies were standard procedure. He next turned up on the high wire in a Berlin circus and then as an artist's model outside of Paris. Needing money, he subsidized his artistic studies by posing as a painter's model. "My young body was dedicated to the progress of art," he informs us. Soon his young body attracted the attention of Auguste Rodin, and before long he was the great sculptor's favorite physique.

©1917
White
N.Y.

But life with the master grew dull and Tellegen was soon off to become a knife thrower in Montmartre and to defeat the world's champion wrestler in a knife fight. The call of the stage then sounded in his breast and he occupied himself with drama until he met the Countess de V—— who paid his way to Constantinople, where he won two hundred thousand dollars at the gambling tables. Traveling on to Bombay, he met a Hindu devoted to the study of Buddhism (he does not qualify this paradox) who took him to the Himalayas. "Women! Women!" cried the Hindu-Buddhist, as Tellegen whistled at the ladies. "Raise your eyes to heaven, to the Himalayas! There you will find beauty and tranquillity."

From Bombay to Cairo, where our hero is having a love bout at the foot of the pyramids. Then to Granada, where he becomes a bullfighter under the name of "Martinez," lives in a castle overlooking the Alhambra, and passes the time "roaming the foliage of the narrow serpertine mountains with the adorable Pepita, whose figure was like that of a Tanagra." When he loses Pepita to white slavers he moves to Paris, becomes an intimate of Isadora Duncan and a friend of Sardou and Caruso, and enjoys a short affair with a German spy. This relationship ends abruptly when Tellegen returns home one evening to find his frau smoking cigars and heaving champagne bottles in a lesbian free-for-all with Mata Hari.

By now Tellegen has lost his fortune, sold his villa, and returned to the stage where women loved his frilled shirts and his passionate delivery, a throwback to the cape-swinging era.

He made a great reputation on stage and between performances studied sculpture with the German master Bourdelle. Under the German's tutelage one of his statues was accepted by the Louvre; a great honor, he assures us. In Paris he also met Mimosa, "a stately creature, voluptuous, extremely well formed, imposing, with a head like Medusa, black hair, beautiful hazel eyes, full red lips, and a smile that evoked passion." She was a peculiar woman who never went outdoors, covered her windows with heavy draperies, and in some convoluted manner managed to have Tellegen framed and sentenced to five years in prison.

Miraculously cleared in a retrial that was the talk of Paris, Tellegen tired of French life and traveled to South America. He headed for the Amazonian jungles and at this point his pseudo-anthropological narrative reaches the outer limits as he tells how he battled with "the perils of death, snakes, poison insects, yellow

Scenes from Queen Elizabeth *with Sarah Bernhardt and Lou Tellegen.*

fever, and the spears of native 'bushmen.' " A return to civilization and a romance with the Princess of Aracaju, a junket to Rio and another affair, a stint as a snake charmer with some wandering Algerian Arabs, and back to France on a trump steamer shoveling coal with eleven hostile Africans. On returning to Paris he was introduced to Sarah Bernhardt.

There is, in fact, no doubt that Bernhardt was infatuated with Tellegen. She was then sixty-nine years old, but he tells us that she looked twenty-five and here he probably does not exaggerate, for many of her contemporaries made the same observation. He signed a four-year contract with Bernhardt and left for America, and together they toured the New World, moving across the plains in Madame Sarah's private railroad train.

Although he lived in the same car with her, Tellegen always denied the gossip that came of this cohabitation. Bernhardt, however, was not reluctant to tell the world how she adored her Lou. She gave him top billing, insisted on his company everywhere, called him *assassin* at times and *mon enfant* at others, and for years scarcely let him out of her sight.

Then in 1912 Bernhardt announced that movies were her only chance for immortality and made a film in France called *Queen Elizabeth*. In this picture Tellegen was the leading man. Adolph Zukor, a founder of Paramount and the man who would soon lure the greatest stage actors to films in his Famous Players in Famous Plays series, purchased the American rights to *Queen Elizabeth*. Bernhardt in a movie, he reasoned, was just the thing to make the cinema respectable. He was right. The film opened at the Lyceum Theater in New York and for the first time in film history members of the "best sets" came en masse, their arrival helping to wean the cinema from its dependence on lower-class patronage and the nickel admissions.

Tellegen, from his association with *Queen Elizabeth,* became a prestige item and producers started wooing him. After a brief run in a play called *Taking Chances,* which was closed down on a morals charge, he signed with Samuel Goldwyn.

It is difficult to realize how popular Tellegen's films were at one time, so completely have they disappeared today. He was total "class," a gen–u–ine French import with Old Country cape-and-sword credentials. He was to films in his time what Laurence Olivier is to them today, something altogether special, something only for those who appreciate the best and finest in life. In *Lust for Gold* he played a French-Canadian landowner who meets his old love in the wilderness. The usual romantic entanglements ensue. "His kisses," a reviewer said, "are still the perfect culmination of all the romance in the world." "When he appears and smiles," said another, "we know that he is not only the greatest of lovers, the greatest of actors, but the most handsome of them all as well." Then in *The Blue Devil* Tellegen was a French officer who finds intrigue and love on a tour of the United States. "Splendid! Wonderful!" cried a critic. "French romance, hand-kissing romance, dashing romance, it lives again with Tellegen." And another: "Theatergoers who are looking to find love's young dream in the excess will find that Lou Tellegen justifies all the languishing things women say about him."

In 1916 Tellegen made *Maria Rosa,* playing a villain opposite Geraldine Farrar, the opera singer turned actress. A romance developed and the next year they were married, becoming one of the most written-about couples in pictures. For a time Tellegen could do no wrong and was pursued by what one actor called "obstinate success." But when Mrs. Tellegen insisted on being billed above her husband, and when Mr. Tellegen insisted on being billed above his wife, the marriage went distinctly sour. In 1921 an ugly divorce case broke, one of the earliest in films to receive international coverage, and the couple separated in a burst of name-calling, bitterness, and heavy litigation.

By the early 1920's Tellegen began to lose his looks and then his audience, and although he remained in films almost up to the talkies he was really old stuff before they arrived. In 1934 the once-

Geraldine Farrar

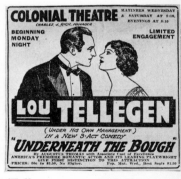

Tellegen was one of the few actors who simultaneously maintained a career on stage and in film. His plays, like his films, were, of course, romances.

• 95

Prior to the Pickford-Fairbanks marriage, Lou Tellegen and Geraldine Farrar were the most famous couple in Hollywood. Their divorce filled the papers for months, and accusations on both sides became so virulent that even the scandal sheets balked at reprinting some of their mutual slanders.

great lover tried a stage comeback—by now he was penniless—and when it failed he committed suicide by stabbing himself to death with a pair of rusty scissors.

The Patriotic Matinee Idol

DOUGLAS FAIRBANKS

"He comes in with a grin," begins the newspaper article, "jumps over a chair, turns three handsprings, two flips, and a somersault before shaking hands. While you are asking him where he was born he breaks a bucking horse and does a little fancy two-gun

Douglas Fairbanks

shooting. Between answers to your questions he runs a foot race, kicks the chandelier, and puts the hammerlock on a giant. And no matter what he is doing, or where he is doing it, he is traveling like a ninety-horsepower, twenty-six-cylinder racing auto. Yes, friends, it's Douglas Fairbanks. Let him perform."

Let him perform. It was 1918 and Fairbanks, at the height of his career, was working hard to raise one million dollars for the war effort. He posed for publicity shots atop a skyscraper holding Charlie Chaplin on his shoulders and hung upside-down out of a railroad car window, greasing the wheels of a liberty train. In New York City he shouted up from the streets to J. Pierpont Morgan's office and asked him to drop a check out the window, leaped over subway kiosks for the benefit of the crowds, and climbed into the windows of the austere Union Club to solicit contributions. Photographs of him in boxing gloves, knocking out the Kaiser, were plastered over the windows of department stores, and when a sixteen-year-old boy named Thomas Rhodes offered him one million dollars for lessons in gymnastics, Fairbanks thought only of his country. "That's great," he told Rhodes, "but you're too liberal with your money. You invest that amount in Liberty Bonds and I will teach you the stunts as a compliment to your generosity."

To increase the fund drive, Fairbanks organized a colossal rodeo in San Francisco. A two-hundred-cowboy marching band playing "When Johnny Comes Marching Home" led the parade of patriotic personalities into the arena, followed by thirty girls in Red Cross uniforms who held up signs showing dollar bills and American eagles. The Bevo ponies, a prize-winning team owned by the Anheuser-Busch Brewing Company, were loaned for the occasion and pulled a chariot of more Red Cross girls who smilingly tossed contribution forms into the audience. Next came the world's champion bucking-horse rider, Prairie Rue, followed by three Hollywood starlets dressed in chicken suits holding a mock cockfight in the center of the stadium; the crescendo of the spectacle came when a certain Tote DuCrow entered the fracas dressed as a chanticleer and pecked the three quarreling chickens out of the ring. Cowboys and cowgirls entered the show and danced a quadrille on horseback while the band marched in different formations and played patriotic tunes, and finally the moment everyone was waiting for arrived: into the center of the arena, amidst pandemonium in the grandstands, rode the master of ceremonies, Douglas Fairbanks, doing a handstand on top of his automobile

IN "THE MAN OF THE HOUR"

◄◄◄◄◄◄ ▶▶▶▶▶▶

IN "ALL FOR A GIRL"

MR. DOUGLAS FAIRBANKS

DOUGLAS FAIRBANKS is generally regarded as the leading exponent of light comedy boys and young men of to-day. He has an ingratiating personality charged with health, directness, breeziness, and a certain patrician quality which contributes an attraction to any part he plays. He has been on the stage only nine years, yet in that time he has created a new rôle in New York on an average of at least once a year.

Mr. Fairbanks was born in Colorado and went on the stage in 1899, in support of Frederick Warde, playing small parts in that actor's Shakespearian repertoire. He soon doffed the romantic costume, however, and has since been seen only in modern dress. He made his début at the Manhattan Theatre in 1900, in support of Herbert Kelcey and Effie Shannon as the young lover, Lord Canning, in Martha Morton's "Her Lord and Master." The play passed and Fairbanks remained. The next season he acted small parts in "The Rose of Plymouth Town" and "Mrs. Jack."

Landry Court was the first character in which he had a real chance to score and he attained a fixed position by his performance of it. This was in Channing Pollock's dramatization of Frank Norris's "The Pit," in Wilton Lackaye's company in the spring of 1904. He played in "Two Little Sailor Boys," and when "Fantana" ran at the Lyric, he took his first and last dip into musical comedy.

The next time he appeared he was "featured" in "A Case of Frenzied Finance." It was not for long. A part in "As Ye Sow" reacquainted him with touring in 1905. During the summer of 1906 he acted a round of juvenile parts in one of the summer stock companies for which Denver has for many years been famous, and when he returned to New York in the fall he created Thomas Smith, Jr., with Grace George in "Clothes." Two of his most conspicuous hits sandwiched in his successive appearances as Perry Carter Wainwright in "The Man of the Hour," as a star in "All for a Girl" and playing the secretary as a co-star with Thomas A. Wise in "A Gentleman From Mississippi."

IN "A GENTLEMAN FROM MISSISSIPPI"

IN "A CASE OF FRENZIED FINANCE"

A rare photo of Fairbanks in his stage years, as usual, surrounded by girls.

Long before he entered films Fairbanks was a top stage comedian, a protegé of James J. Corbett's manager, William Brady. He had no intention of entering films until a roving cinematographer photographed him turning cartwheels in New York's Central Park and sent the footage to California. A Hollywood contract was forthcoming.

and kissing the stars and stripes painted on the hood.

It was part of Fairbanks' greatness that he never did anything in a small way. Every generation creates its heroes in the image of the times, and he was the American superman of his day, larger than life, larger than any American or any human being could ever be; indeed, the likes of him have never been seen again on the great silver screen.

He was born in Denver, Colorado, and spent his youth wan-

Fairbanks in His Majesty the American, *made in 1919. For wooing scenes Doug preferred walls, trees, window ledges, and eagle nests to more conventional locations. Courtesy, United Artists*

dering through a dozen occupations. He did a short stint at Harvard and a shorter one as a stockbroker, and finally ended up in the theater. At twenty-one, as the lead in *Frenzied Finance* in the year 1908, he was the theater's youngest male star, and for ten years more was the leading exponent of polite comedy and light romance.

By 1915 he had left the east as part of a mass migration of stage personalities from New York to Hollywood, an exodus that included such stars as George Arliss, George M. Cohan, De Wolf Hopper, the Barrymore family, and Nazimova. This drain of talent so depleted New York's dramatic resources that the legitimate theater never really recovered from the shock and became a big attraction again only when the age of the great Broadway musicals began.

Like other refugees from the theater, Fairbanks was dubious about films. But he had been offered a position with D. W. Griffith's Triangle Studios and could hardly refuse. The price was right, twenty-five hundred dollars a week, and ever since he had seen Griffith's *Birth of a Nation* he was fascinated by the great director. "I never spent any evening more thrilling, entertaining, or instructional than when I saw *Birth of a Nation*," he once said, when asked why he entered pictures. "I went four or five nights consecutively. Till then I had never thought of going to films—my ambition was to be another Booth!"

At Triangle the great Griffith turned out to be a fastidious taskmaster with little love for overpriced stage prima donnas and none for the flippant Fairbanks. He buried him in lackluster make-up for his first picture, *The Lamb,* and finally ignored him completely. Things looked bad until a director named John Emerson and a script writer named Anita Loos (later to become famous for *Gentlemen Prefer Blondes*) picked him up and put him in a string of snappy romance-comedies.

These Loos films and others like them brought out the quintessential Fairbanks style which Griffith had never recognized, and established a personality formula which he used until the 20's. The ingredients of this formula were attuned to the self-image of the American male and the dreams of his screen-struck girlfriend. The man of action was everybody's idol, and here was Fairbanks to enact him, the modern motor-driven, superelectric dynamo lover, the man compulsively on the go. His lovemaking as this character combined the maturity of a man over thirty with a little-boyish quality which women could scarcely resist. His acrobatics in these roles, with their tremendous masculine appeal, have never been equaled on film. "You can't keep a squirrel or

When portraying the hotshot entrepreneur with seventeen desk telephones, Fairbanks, in real life a brilliant businessman, was in his element. He is shown below in a movie with the appropriately aggressive and competitive title, Reaching for the Moon. *Courtesy, United Artists*

Though not directly identified with the western tradition of William S. Hart and Tom Mix, Fairbanks nevertheless made cowboy films and found them "funny—and wonderful, always." Courtesy, United Artists

Douglas Fairbanks on the ground," the press said, and mothers complained that their children were destroying the furniture and falling out of trees trying to imitate his stunts. He dashed across cliffs to save young ladies and plunged into the ocean with all his clothes on. Advertisements for *The Mollycoddle* showed him hanging in midair halfway between a cliff and the top of a tree. He scaled apartment buildings like a human fly, escaped from dangerous predicaments on conveyor belts, and once shot himself into the air using a tree limb as a slingshot. It was a point of principle for him to do these feats himself and never once would he use a stuntman. "They might get hurt," he said.

Complementing these heroics was Fairbanks' famous prescription for living. "Never say die," he repeated a hundred times in "Doug's Recipe," a syndicated newspaper column in which he outlined his sanguine philosophy· "Laugh at your work and make it easy—start the day with a smile—the greatest thing in this little old world is enthusiasm—have that unconquerable spirit of enterprise that laughs at reverses, takes obstacles as something to whet the appetite for further endeavors, and fights for what it wants for the pure joy of fighting." In picture after picture he followed his own advice: through hard work and persistent optimism he rose from obscurity to win the girl and a million too, making his movies subliminal sermons for the rags-to-riches dream of the common American man. The fact that in real life he was one of the most uncommon men in America, a sensational-looking, athletic, brainy financier who earned a salary nine times greater than the president of the United States, in no way detracted from his image as a good average Joe. This was Fairbanks' ultimate magic: he sold himself as a typical American male and then made this American male into a demigod, thereby flattering a nation by making the normal seem extraordinary and the supernormal seem ordinary.

Fairbanks was a great advocate of motion picture art and pushed it every chance he could get. "Pictures are educational, instructive, reasonable, and contain profound reform possibilities," he said. "They keep a man at home with his family and in line with prohibition theories, a great thing for any community." In 1918, when he was making seven movies a year, a threat to his image both as film sponsor and family man developed when rumors of a coming divorce were circulated through Hollywood. "The story is false," he told the press, "just a piece of German propaganda." But that year he left his wife and soon announced his engagement to the greatest of all film stars of the day, "Little" Mary Pickford.

On the eve of the Jazz Age, in 1920, with the blessings of a country that couldn't hold a grudge against such a perfect union, they were married, and on their honeymoon through Europe they were swamped in every country. Doug was photographed standing on his head in front of a Gothic cathedral—he was forever standing on his head—and became the American businessman for a moment by sending word home that "the movie industry is far behind the times here. American initiative is what's needed to stir competition among continental producers." Mary, whose films were beloved in Europe, was innundated with crowds of worshippers in London and Paris. "Outside the window we saw them," Pickford recalled in her autobiography, "thousands and thousands of them, waiting day and night in the streets below, just for a glimpse of us."

In all history only two other Americans, Eisenhower and Lindbergh, would be so well received on the Continent.

The couple returned to America and were welcomed at the dock by Jack Dempsey, who arranged a six-motorcycle escort for them in an automobile decked out with American flags. Returning to Hollywood, they moved to a suburb of Los Angeles called

Douglas Fairbanks and Mary Pickford in The Taming of the Shrew. *Courtesy, United Artists*

Fairbanks in The Mark of Zorro. *Courtesy, United Artists*

Beverly Hills and made it a chic place to live. At their beautiful new home which they called "Pickfair," they built a swimming pool a hundred feet long, starting a craze for home pools which has possessed Hollywood citizens ever since. They were the topic of popular songs and endless gossip. They ate at the White House with Woodrow Wilson and entertained kings and queens. Then, because they couldn't get more than a million dollars a year from their respective studios, they formed their own, United Artists, and Fairbanks began producing his own pictures.

It was now 1921 and the bloody war had soured the public on Fairbanks' goodie-goodie films, so he turned to the production of costume dramas. By 1920 he had already made *The Mark of Zorro*, based on a weekly serial called *The Curse of Capistrano* which had appeared in the *All Story Weekly*. It was a tale about a Spanish youth, Don Diego Vega, who lived in nineteenth-century California and posed as an indolent imbecile, much to the consternation of his father and his beautiful fiancée. But in reality he was Zorro, a Robin Hood of the Spanish west, who righted wrongs behind a black mask and left his calling card by cutting the letter "Z" into the face of any desperado unlucky enough to cross swords with him. *The Mark of Zorro* was Fairbanks' first period romance, and it was such a success that in 1921 he grew a mustache (which he never shaved off) to play D'Artagnan in *The Three Musketeers,* built the largest movie-set castle ever constructed in 1922 for *Robin Hood,* and starred in *The Thief of Bagdad* in 1924 and in *Don Q. Son of Zorro* in 1925. But beneath these new swashbuckling parts and the flowing French and Spanish capes, the familiar Doug, the daredevil, the indefatigable all-around romantic Doug, was always discernible beneath the disguise, and so he remained until he bade adieu to films forever.

Courtesy, United Artists

Looking back over Fairbanks' glamorous career it is clear that he, along with Mary Pickford, was the chief catalyst of the glamorization process of the movies, the one who gave shape and definition to the Hollywood dream. He and Pickford lived in such magnificent houses, knew such fascinating personalities, were beloved by so many millions of people, made so much money and were, at least to the public eye, so ecstatically happy with it all, that they star-struck a nation. They fashioned the filmland myth, molded it and gave it apparent substance until, like some magician's conjury, it sparkled high in the air like an ancient jeweled treasure before the eyes of the world. If, after all, it was just an illusion, an ornate cardboard set with only bare scaffolds and empty space behind it, this fact was unknown beyond the charmed circle, unknown to all the pretty girls and hopeful young men who packed their fiberboard suitcases and headed west, each hoping to find there a real-life reenactment of the great glamorous fable they had seen Douglas Fairbanks portray so many times on and off the great silver screen.

Fairbanks in The Black Pirate. *Courtesy, United Artists*

WILLIAM S. HART
& TOM MIX

As the real wild west closed at the beginning of the twentieth
century a celluloid one arose to take its place. Early screen versions
of the frontier were not, however, the fairy-tale "modern" westerns
we know today; they were grassroots sagas that told it, at least to
some extent, like it was. Such authenticity was due in no part to
the efforts of the first screen cowboy, Broncho Billy Anderson, who
in 1903 brought to his films such total ignorance of the range that
three men were enlisted to fit him on his horse for his first western
(and the first real feature film ever made), *The Great Train
Robbery*.

Honors for the preservation of the western tradition belong
to the second screen cowboy, William S. Hart, who in the beginning not only kept the shoot-'em-up close to its origins but introduced dozens of plots and character types that became the brick
and mortar of the western format.

Hart himself was once a real cowboy. He had been raised in
the Dakotas near a Sioux reservation and could speak Sioux almost
as soon as he could walk. He watched them bury his baby brother
on the prairies, worked as a cowpuncher in Kansas, witnessed gun-
fights, hangings, stampedes, range wars. He lived out many of the
stories he was later to dramatize.

Finally he drifted east and became an actor. He was well
known to New York audiences and played his greatest role as
Messala in the stage version of *Ben Hur*, a part that Francis X.
Bushman would later popularize in films. Lured to Hollywood like
so many other stage actors, he was offended by directors who were
already prettifying the west and manipulating reality to please
popular taste. He corrected this false face by directing and acting
in dozens of one- and two-reel westerns for Mutual and Triangle
studios, and at the same time introduced motifs which became
classical ingredients: the fight in the saloon, the faithful horse,

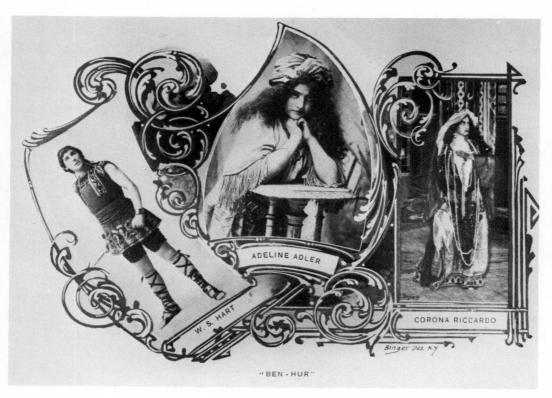

ADELINE ADLER

W. S. HART

CORONA RICCARDO

Singer Des. N.Y.

"BEN-HUR"

Hart, as he looked playing Messala in the stage production of Ben Hur. *The brainchild of Lew Wallace, a Civil War general and member of the court that tried the conspirators in the Lincoln murder, Ben Hur was made into one play, three movies, and in 1928 ranked first behind the Bible as the best-selling book of all time.*

the dude who goes west, the wrangler who comes east, the sheriff who cleans up the boom town, the showdown, the trip west in a covered wagon, the Indian protagonist, and so on down the long list which time has transformed into clichés.

Hart employed few professional actors, preferring to cast with local types picked up on location; through his films walk real Indians, gamblers, prospectors, cowpunchers, and saloon-hall entertainers. In seeing these extras one is still impressed with their faces—they are the McCoy, no makeup, no Hollywood suntans. Their sorrowful and disarmingly powerful features, weathered into rawness by the desert sun, stare out at audiences and speak with a fluency more vivid than much of the best of so-called *cinema verité.*

Not handsome in a classic sense, Hart nevertheless had an arresting face, long and angular like a cigar-store Indian's, and he put it to good romantic use. His films inevitably contained a sentimental and highly emotional love story. In the beginning, western films such as *The Great Train Robbery* and a number of other Broncho Billy Anderson specials had no romantic interest in them at all. But films were a commercial animal from the start, romance meant good box office, and Hart was one of the first to capitalize on this demand.

His love stories usually involved a transformation theme. In one version of this theme he was the misanthropic outlaw in love with some garden-fresh Sunbonnet Sue, the rancher's-daughter-just-returned-from-finishing-school-in-the-east. Through her goodness this untarnished virgin reformed him and he embraced the straight-and-narrow and her with it In a variation on this theme, Hart was the redeemer and his subject some thick-hided but beautiful saloon girl whose reformation involved little enough tenderness. He beat her up, whalloped her, pulled her hair, threw her across the room when she was unfaithful, and bullied her when she got high-minded. These bad-girls-turned-good stories sometimes had tragic endings—the reformed lady steps in front

In a Hart movie there were two kinds of women, good ones and bad ones. Here he hesitatingly shakes hands with a good one; hesitating because he is cowed by her sublime virtue.

of a bullet with Hart's name on it and dies in his arms—and this was something unique among the thousands of happy endings rolling off the cinematic production lines.

Hart used such love stories time and again. Not young when he began in films, the inflexibility of middle age soon showed in both his face and in his refusal to change the format of his films. Bored, the fans turned their fickle eyes to another cowboy named . . .

Tom Mix was everything Hart was not. He wore a frilly cowboy suit and flamboyant ten-gallon hat which made Hart's simple leather trousers seem ragged in comparison. Hart would cinematically shoot to kill, as it was really done in the west, but Mix only grazed the bad guys, knicked the top of their heads so they "fainted" long enough to bring them in for a fair trial. In his private life Hart was circumspect, humorless, with never a breath of scandal attached to his name. Mix, on the other hand, courted notoriety. On the front lawn of his enormous ranch a neon sign flashed "Tom Mix" in blue letters. He drove through Hollywood in a Rolls Royce with a pair of antlers as a radiator cap, and once ordered tires for his limousine with his initials printed on them in relief. Hollywood then had dirt roads so wherever

Tom Mix and his horse, Tony.

he drove he left a long trail of T.M.'s imprinted behind him in the dust. He was the first cowboy to introduce the automobile to a western, bringing the hard-driving as well as the hard-riding hero to the flicks (eventually he would die in a motor accident by driving his car into a tree), and in the minds of a public that wanted its stars to be sensationalists, he was everything a cowboy ought in fact to be as the Roaring Twenties approached.

But Mix was no cream puff. He had been a Texas Ranger and a Rough Rider with Roosevelt, a deputy marshal and champion rodeo rider. When he rented his Oklahoma ranch to the Selig Film Company, Selig liked his style so much that they offered him a contract. In 1918 he left Selig and went to Fox—Hart was then already on the decline—and with Fox's power to push and promote behind him he soon became number-one cowboy.

Mix, the first cowboy to turn auto racer, gets his due from man and woman alike for winning the thrilling race (left). Hand-holding romance, Mix variety. Later such romantic scenes were intentionally injected into most cowboy pictures to allow the male juveniles in the audience, not romantically inclined, to storm the popcorn concessions, usually owned by the studios that produced the movie. Courtesy, 20th Century-Fox

Hart punches a villain in Tumbleweeds. *Despite the ludicrous posed quality of this shot,* Tumbleweeds *is considered one of the greatest westerns ever made. Courtesy, United Artists*

If Hart brought romantic interest to the western, Mix took it away. Action spoke louder than love in Mix's vocabulary, a fact which lost him some female support but gained him an empire of grammar-school males. Women became incidental ornaments in his films, things to be rescued from holdout shacks at the end of the pictures and made eyes at in between. He never kissed a girl in his films. This was his firm rule and he never disobeyed it. He might hold the girl's hand while he sat with her on the fence, swinging his legs dreamily as his omnipresent steed Tony grazed in the pastures behind, but physical contact rarely went beyond this point. "I may be foreman of the ranch and I may get the girl," he once said, "but there is never a fervid love scene."

Mix established a formula for the sexless western that lasted into the 1950's when the new realism returned it a little in films like *High Noon* and *Shane*. Cowboys from Hoot Gibson and Ken Maynard to Roy Rogers and Gene Autry were all heir to the Mix flirt-and-run legacy, and these Mixian heroes, to the glee of youngsters who bought comic books and cap guns embossed with their names, were more infatuated with horses and pearl-handled revolvers than with their leading ladies.

William S. Hart sensed that in the wake of this new breed his time had come. In 1926 he made his last picture, *Tumbleweeds*. Considered a classic today, it received mixed reactions and Hart retired to his ranch in southern California, only rarely returning to Hollywood. There he watched, with what emotions we can only guess, as the new generation of cowboys with their tight pants and shiny guitars completed the work of distorting the facts as they had been west of the Great Divide, before the fable-maker called the motion picture.

The All-American Matinee Idol

WALLACE REID

Wallace Reid might have made the perfect F. Scott Fitzgerald character, a Dick Diver or even a Gatsby, an eighteen-karat-gold Princeton man—flaming, gentle, beautiful, and doomed. He even looked a bit like Fitzgerald and was his contemporary. But Fitzgerald's characters were heirs to the world and its contaminations. Reid was not, at least on the screen. For he was the primordial innocent of movieland.

In a time before Valentino brought his brooding, troubled image to the photodrama, the matinee idol had a sort of naïveté about him which was given classic depiction by Reid. Even when he dressed in a tuxedo or a barbarian's helmet, which he often did, there was something in his manner which said just-plain-folks. People found this appealing, reassuring, even relaxing. If a woman didn't want him for a lover she wanted him for a son. To reinforce this ingenuous image Reid continually posed for homey

The American dream of innocent love was in Wallace Reid's day the supreme romantic mode in films and popular music. Although Reid was its premier proponent, dozens of other incorruptible young men from Thomas Meighan and Jack Holt to Neil Hamilton, Charles Ray and Richard Barthelmess were similarly in the forefront.

publicity snapshots. On a picket fence he sat reading the local newspaper or in an overstuffed chair he smoked a pipe before the hearth or on a precariously balanced kitchen stool he reached to stir a pot of soup while he studied his script. "He's the kind of man who fills his wife's boudoir with roses," said one article. "Wally knows that a cheerful grin will get you in, a frown will get you down," said another. "My chief hobbies are my little son, surgery, and music," said Reid himself. So perfectly did this domestic symbolism click with the contemporary mentality that by 1918 Reid was the top nice guy of motion pictures.

He *was* a nice guy. Everyone who knew him said so. Quiet, modest, clean, happy, serious about all his roles but never demanding, father of an adopted child, his list of virtues read like

• 115

Thomas Meighan (left), for years the gentle star of innumerable uncomplicated romances. Courtesy, Warner Brothers

Neil Hamilton (right) as the Arrow Collar man.

Neil Hamilton (below). Originally discovered by D. W. Griffith, his face was soon known off screen as the Arrow Collar man, a later version of the Gibson man. Courtesy, Paramount Pictures

the Boy Scout oath. He was also the most handsome man in films. His "million-dollar eyes" gazed out from the screen with a glance that was piercing and langorous as well. "He lifts one eye now," said *Theater* magazine, "and sighs of admiration echo through the darkened house; he arches them both, and every woman is at his feet."

It was his chameleonlike versatility as well as his appearance which kept Reid on top. With his all-American-boy looks, he pleased the antiforeign sentiments of pre-World War I America, and when war broke out his aptness at filling up uniforms in patriotic plots made him the ideal picture of all the boys "over there." War ended and Reid became the male flapper, the dancing fool (in these dance pictures he was advertised with such slick but meaningless phrases as "he's jazzing the jug business by day and jugging the jazz business by night"), the playboy, the dynamist, the young tycoon on the rise, the race car driver.

Particularly the race car driver. The automobile was still a novelty in 1921 and film audiences as well as adolescent speedsters had just realized that the family jalopy could be used for fun as well as transportation, *Watch My Speed, Excuse My Dust, Roaring Road, Too Much Speed, What's Your Hurry, The Love Special,* and *Double Speed* were all bonanzas on wheels, were all made in one year, 1921, and were all advertised with such hard-pounding, acceleration-stressing copy as "A ninety-mile-an-hour knockout," "A rough-riding rolling romance that runs on love and spurts blue flames of excitement," and "A record-shattering, extra-dynamic electric lightning-charged super sock-'em-o of a film!"

Reid came to motion pictures by accident. His original ambition had been to learn cinematography, but when his father, Hal Reid, an actor-writer of the earliest days of film, introduced his handsome nineteen-year-old son around the lots, it was only a matter of time before he was signed for pictures. Jesse Lasky's eagle eye saw him playing a G-string Indian role for Selig and a blacksmith in *Birth of a Nation,* and Lasky quickly offered him a contract with Famous Players. "He was," said Lasky, "the most

Richard Barthelmess (right), the ideal hero—modest, unassuming, handsome. His most beloved role was David, the country boy, in Tol'able David. The title of this film derived from David's dauntless efforts to prove himself to his pioneer mother, who at the end of the film conceded he was "Tol'able, [tolerable] David, tol'able."

Jack Holt (below left), a two-fisted, no-nonsense straight guy, always big money at the box office. Courtesy, Paramount Pictures

Charles Ray (below), king of the hicks, star of such folksy films as Home, The Clodhopper, The Old Swimmin' Hole, The Busher (pictured), and The Village Sleuth.

Romance, Wallace Reid style (left), with sweet girl in bonnet and friendly dog. Courtesy, Paramount Pictures

In 1922 all men wore attachable collars. But when Reid (below) put on a soft white shirt minus the stiff neckpiece as shown, most collar companies went out of business. Courtesy, Paramount Pictures

Reid (below right), atypically unshaven, has just been shanghaied and cast aboard ship bound for South America in Always Audacious. Courtesy, Paramount Pictures

charming, personable, handsome young man I've ever known, and the most cooperative."

Producers traditionally love cooperative actors. They are or were so easily taken advantage of. Lasky exploited and reexploited Reid's willingness to work and starred him in a drama a month. By 1921, above Charles Ray and Thomas Meighan, he was voted the top male star of the cinema. But rank had its price. A merciless schedule and millions of demanding fans were wearing him down, and the studios, eager to service the public's voracious appetite for romance à la Reid, allowed him almost no time to rest between films.

One day on the set Reid's head was cut open in a freak accident and the doctor prescribed morphine to relieve the pain of eleven stitches. It turned out to be just what was needed to calm him from the listless malaise brought on by pressure and exhaustion, and soon he was taking daily portions of the drug. In the next eighteen months he became a confirmed morphine user. For the first time in his career he grew uncooperative and failed to show up for work. At first people thought that fame had finally gone to his head, but soon the real cause was discovered and it became the worst-kept secret in Hollywood that Reid was an addict. Realizing that his career was at stake, he entered a sanitarium, vowing that

he would come back cured or not at all. He kept his promise. Drug dissipation and the agonies of withdrawal had weakened his resistance and he died of influenza.

This sorry finis to the life of the all-American boy happened to come at the time Fatty Arbuckle was on trial for the rape-murder of a young starlet, Virginia Rappe, and from both sides of the continent the rubber finger shame-shamed filmland. Muckrakers cried for an antinarcotics law and a league of decency to patrol the infested Hollywood quagmires. The Motion Picture Producers and Distributors League was founded to monitor films and, in Washington, Reid's death contributed to new narcotic legislation. But in Hollywood, except for a few ethical modifications, things remained pretty much the way they had always been. Reid was cremated and his funeral kept the reporters in movement for a while. Hundreds flocked to the doors of the chapel to catch sight of the glamorous bereaved. William S. Hart, Jack Holt, and Conrad Nagel, among others, were the pallbearers, and inside the casket lay Reid, dressed in a simple tweed suit.

Perhaps it was best that he died young, for just around the corner was one who would make them all pass into the shadows.

The Exotic Matinee Idol

RUDOLPH VALENTINO

In 1921 the typical box office hero was still of the Wallace Reid ilk, a mom's apple-pie boy running wingback for State U. or winning the automobile race for his future father-in-law. On the surface audiences seemed pleased with this type, but an astute observer might have sensed a restlessness, a desire for change. Nevertheless, movie studios were conservative, content to mine a formula as long as it worked. Why rock the boat? So when a swarthy Italian actor named Valentino came on the scene in 1918 he was glanced over by the casting directors, marked as a decidedly non-American type, and relegated to the bad guy department.

Valentino in The Four Horsemen of the Apocalypse. *Courtesy, MGM Studios. Rudolph Valentino as the sheik. Courtesy, Paramount Pictures.*

For Valentino, playing the heavy was not exactly typecasting, although as a boy he had gotten into enough scrapes with the Italian police to warrant a trip in steerage to America. He arrived here in 1913 with plans to be an agricultural engineer, but his aspirations brought him only as far as the parterres and walkways of New York's Central Park, which he swept with resentment, and a room in a Times Square flophouse. "My hotel room at Forty-third and Broadway was a skylight cubbyhole for storing brooms," he recalled. "I washed in a mop sink, dried on newspaper, and could not raise two dollars weekly rental. Next came a twelve-cent-a-night room and then a Central Park bench."

In New York Valentino found himself drawn to the hot spots, the cabarets and all-night bars, and finally became a gigolo at Maxims. Courting dance-crazed dowagers, he earned ten-dollar tips and eventually collected enough to travel west, but in San Francisco destitution drove him back to café society with its eager and prosperous widows.

One day while visiting Hollywood he met up with an old friend, Norman Kerry, who had become a successful leading man in the movies. Kerry suggested films to Valentino and helped him get his first part as a walk-on in *Alimony*. For three years he played assorted gangsters and thugs. Then in 1921 Metro procured the rights to Blasco Ibáñez's famous antiwar novel, *The Four Horsemen of the Apocalypse,* and announced they were searching for a foreign type to play the role of Julio, an Argentinian youth who goes to war to redeem his father's cowardly name. June Mathis, the writer assigned to the project, had been watching Valentino for two years and insisted that he get the part. Metro was skeptical of using such an obviously foreign character and they remained skeptical until the film opened to rave reviews. Valentino then made *Camille* with the great Russian star Nazimova, then *The Conquering Power,* and finally *The Sheik.*

The Sheik began as something of a throwaway for Paramount, and ended up revolutionizing the film business and sections of American culture with it. Today scenes from *The Sheik* make us

Valentino in The Eagle, *the perfect externalization of a primary female fantasy. Courtesy, United Artists.*

The two Valentinos, the overbearing lover and the winsome boy.

laugh. We watch as Valentino bulges his eyes at Agnes Ayres, walks around her like a dog circling a veal cutlet, and pulls her headfirst into his tent. But to audiences in 1921 this type of insistent seduction was unique. Certainly neither Fairbanks nor Reid had ever dragged a woman into a pleasure tent—they would never have had such a thing in their pictures—and the likes of Jack Holt or Charles Ray or Richard Barthelmess would have throttled the cad who considered it. It was something novel, a total departure from any love scene ever witnessed on film, and to add to the piquancy of the whole thing was the olive skin, the sensuous oiled hair and sideburns, the penciled eyebrows and gigolo's stare. Soon a vogue for brilliantined hair swept Hollywood and the hair tonic business was transformed into a major industry. Women called their boyfriends "sheiks," and the word became part of the vernacular. In an overnight metamorphosis, sideburns appeared on the temples of a multitude of studio regulars gone Latin, and a horde of foreign emigrants with "bedroom eyes" invaded the Hollywood lots and played in an assortment of mostly B-grade movies featuring

desert backdrops and swarthy heroes in burnooses.

It was apparent that the movies had found the perfect externalization of a primary female fantasy, a collective wish-fulfillment in human form. For the male moviegoers of the day, who found Valentino greasy and effeminate, he was not something to enjoy but to imitate, and this only because the girls demanded it. From the beginning he was a woman's actor and it was women who made him the most popular male entertainer of the twentieth century.

Why this is so has been argued for years. Perhaps it was because he offered women two basic cravings: to take and to be taken, to be both the active lover and the passively loved. He was a master of either extreme. With a robust vitality that sometimes bordered on the sadistic, he would subdue any woman who defied him. Or, if the part demanded, he could be the sensitive and insecure young man, really just a little boy in need of love. Women felt this duality was part of the man himself. "There was a look of unhappiness in his dark eyes," said Pola Negri in her autobiography, "that appealed more to the maternal than to the amo-

Valentino at the gaming table in Camille, *made in 1921 with Nazimova, the Russian stage prima donna-turned-movie star. Courtesy, MGM Studios*

rous. He was rather like a vulnerable child all decked out in fancy clothes." "They would like me to be their son," said Valentino about his fans. "It is the maternal instinct."

But Valentino did not only bring a new model of the lover; he brought a new kind of film to put him in. Heroes were Eagle Scouts fastened to pedestals of virtue until he made them vulnerable. In *Blood and Sand* he plays Gallardo, the most popular bullfighter in Spain and happily married to a devoted wife. Then he meets a beautiful vamp and forsakes everything, even his wife, to crawl after her. A hero never groveled or gave in to the enticements of forbidden flesh, just as he never twisted women's arms or enslaved them in harems. But Valentino was a new man, a susceptible and brutal man, one who could err and did, as any man might do, in the face of overwhelming temptation. Without him the films of Bogart and Cagney and Gable could never have existed. Despite the stiltedness of his style, a style, incidentally, which must be viewed today with the understanding that it is almost fifty years old, he brought a realism to film for which he is rarely credited.

Another part of Valentino's appeal was based on his strange personal life. He was watched by everyone, everywhere. Over two hundred mothers claimed reason to name their children for him. When he grew a beard the barbers' union complained to the film companies: business was falling off at an alarming rate across the country; would the studio persuade him to shave? It was considered sissy to wear a wristwatch, but when Valentino put one on hardly a male wrist was bare. He popularized the waterpipe and Turkish cigarettes, and along with the Prince of Wales, made a vogue of the Tyrolean hat. His life was in the hands of the public, forever taken up with interviews, marriage scandals, disputes with critics, celebrity contests. Everywhere he went an agglomeration of curious faces peered at him through the tinted glass of his limousine, watched him eat his soup at restaurants, tried to snatch the menus out of his hands. Jealous husbands spit on him in public places. Women followed him into the men's room. Hoodlums threw rocks through his hotel room window. "The streets were jumbled with hysterical faces, waving hands, crazy eyes," wrote John Dos Passos in *The Big Money*. "They stuck out their autograph books, yanked his buttons off, cut a tail off his admirablytailored dress suit; they stole his hat and pulled his necktie; his valets removed young women from under his bed; all night in nightclubs and cabarets actresses leching for stardom made sheep'seyes at him under their mascaraed lashes."

Valentino, however, was not quite the sybarite his image purveyed. He did his share of night prowling and womanizing, it's true, although some suggested he enjoyed a plate of ravioli more than the company of women; but in comparison with other male

Starring in Monsieur Beaucaire, *Valentino was made up in laces and rouge, a getup which alienated many male fans and caused a reporter from the* Chicago Tribune *to dub him a pink powderpuff. Courtesy, Paramount Pictures*

stars of his time he was something less than a hedonist, preferring the solitude of his palatial showplace, Falcon's Lair, and the company of his wife, Natacha Rambova. But when Valentino left Paramount to become an independent and his new contract excluded Natacha from any say in his career (she insisted on monitoring all his roles), his ambitious wife deserted him to make her own films, breaking his heart and his health along with it.

In 1926, amidst rumors of his engagement to the actress Pola Negri, the "puff" scandal broke. An unidentified reporter from the Chicago *Tribune* had called him a pink powder puff and suggested that vending machines selling such puffs be installed in men's rooms to service the Valentino vogue. Valentino immediately challenged the unknown calumniator to a fist fight. The culprit would not come forth, but before he could be flushed out in the open Valentino was dead of peritonitis.

He died on August 23, 1926, after five years and five months of glory. His last recorded words were spoken to a doctor near his bedside: "Did I behave like a pink powder puff?"

Courtesy, MGM Studios

The lady in black who visits his grave once a year, the exploitation of his death in such songs as "There's a New Star in Heaven Tonight," and the spinster who sealed his shirt in a golden casket—all are history. One hundred and twenty-five thousand people, mostly women, lined ten city blocks outside the Gold Room of Frank Campbell's Funeral Parlor in New York City to look one last time on his features, powdered, ironically, for the occasion. It was said that to drum up publicity for his unreleased pictures his studio hired women to wail in the crowds and throw themselves under the wheels of his funeral carriage, although the woman who shot herself and left word for her husband that she had gone to join Rudy in heaven was no doubt not included in the put-up.

"The greatest lover in the history of motion pictures and the greatest matinee idol the stage has ever known," was the epicedium penned to him by the Associated Press, and similar words and phrases floated through the ether as long as they sold copy. But some observers who were removed from the immediate hysteria saw the real pathos to be in the drama of a simple and congenial middle-class Italian emigrant who was exploited, swallowed up, and destroyed by the pressures of mass adulation and his own inability to resist them. "A man of relatively civilized feelings," the journalist H. L. Mencken called him. "A man of relatively civilized feelings thrown into a situation of intolerable vulgarity."

Although rarely seen by westerners, the Arab harem with its exotic trappings was a common motif in the American sexual fantasy long before The Sheik. *Here, on a page of sheet music dating from the early part of the twentieth century, beneath oil lamps and hanging velvets, with a blushing concubine at his feet, sits a very Anglo-looking sultan, really just a Gibson man in turban. Such pipedream versions of the Middle East were common in the West even before the nineteenth century.*

RAMON NOVARRO

With the Valentinoizing of the matinee idol a frantic search began here and abroad for suitable Latin types. Scouts canvassed Rome and Florence and traveled to Valentino's home town of Castelleneta to see if there were others like him in the family—there weren't —and even to this day many adolescent males of this town wear greased hair and sideburns and strut conspicuously up and down its craggy streets in hopes that a scout will return to find them.

Meanwhile in Hollywood there was still some confusion over whether a sheik was an Arab or an Italian, although the interested parties didn't quibble, for if they didn't know the name they surely knew the face. Eventually practically every studio had a resident Mediterranean, and even the worst of them, for a time, sold tickets.

Guy Bates Post and Jane Salisbury in the play Omar, the Tentmaker, *another pleasant erotic reverie about life and love in Arabia, produced seven years before Valentino donned his burnoose.*

Antonio Moreno (above left). Courtesy, Paramount Pictures. Norman
Kerry (above right). Ricardo Cortez (left). Monte Blue with Clara
Bow in Kiss Me Again (right). Courtesy, Warner Brothers

Mr. Brewster says: " 'Ben-Hur' seems to clinch my contention that Ramon Novarro bids fair to be the greatest screen idol that has appeared"

Can you figure the man above, with the monocle-mustache combination, a rival to Valentino? Movie makers believe he will prove a counter attraction. He is Ramon Samaniegos, now called Ramon Navarro, juvenile lead in "The Prisoner of Zenda." The heroine is Alice Terry, wife of the director, Rex Ingram.

Antonio Moreno was dragged out of a dying weekly serial and a second-rate career as a second-rate lover, because he had "the look." The dark, Spanish appearance which had been his greatest liability was now his cardinal asset. From Brooklyn came Jake Stein, a young man with stare so intense and eyelids so low and such a quantity of eye white in evidence that Paramount renamed him Ricardo Cortez; and when Valentino walked out on Paramount for the usual reason, money, Jake was pushed with vigor as the miscreant star's replacement. Norman Kerry, the man who brought Valentino to films in the first place, did a brief turn as gigolo. Rod La Rocque was also deemed worthy of shiekdom and pomade. So were Monte Blue and even John Gilbert.

But the most successful of all Valentino's imitators was, amazingly enough, a *real* Latin (Latin American, that is), the only real one, except Moreno, of the lot—Ramon Novarro.

Novarro was born in Durango, Mexico, and fled to America as a child during the Huerta revolution. His name was then Ramón Gil Samaniegos plus eleven honorary titles, none of which helped him or his family to make a living in Hollywood. Coming of age, he went to New York to make his fortune, and ended up a busboy in the Times Square automat. He returned to Hollywood, got a job as an usher at a movie house, and liked to watch films so much that he decided to be in them.

The first years of Novarro's career were spent trying to look the all-American type as later the all-American types would try to

• 135

Ramon Novarro in The Arab. *Courtesy, MGM Studios*

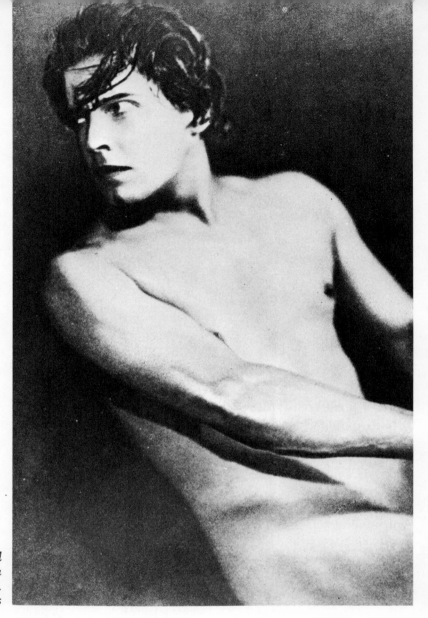

Ramon Novarro, a naked oarsman on the Roman galleys in Ben Hur. *Courtesy, MGM Studios*

look like him. His career went along obscurely enough until someone noticed that he looked enough like Valentino to be, at least, his cousin.

Metro moved quickly. They had found another Rudy in their own backyard and they intended to put him to use. "The Second Valentino" and "Valentino's Greatest Rival," they called him, although he was neither, and starred him in *The Arab*, an unabashed steal from *The Sheik*. Soon the young Mexican occupied a strange niche on the ladder of stardom. He was not the first of movie lovers, for Valentino was decidedly that. Nor was he the second, for that was decidedly John Gilbert. He was the third greatest lover of the screen, an odd distinction; and as such, in all seriousness, he was sometimes billed.

Riding on the Valentino wave, Novarro became known as "Ravishing Ramon," and hawkers on Hollywood Boulevard sold "secret maps" showing the way to his "hidden home." He was in truth a recluse, at least a Hollywood version of one, and his all-black wardrobe, his early bedtime habits, and his annoying custom of minding his own business made him all the more intriguing to fans who wanted to know who he *really* was and what he *really* thought about love. But Novarro insisted on being left alone. "Love is a flame which burns for what it is worth," he said enigmatically to a reporter, and closed his door.

In 1926 Novarro was given the lead role in *Ben Hur*. *Ben Hur* was the most ambitious film that had come out of Hollywood since the days of Griffith's extravaganzas. Its production had traditionally been on a grand scale, and even the stage play had cost its backers more than seventy thousand dollars to produce back in 1899. Metro was making it (actually it had been made into a movie on a much smaller scale by the Kalem Company in 1907) and they sent a

Novarro in costume with Alice Terry (left). With patent leather hair, à la Valentino, Ramon Novarro appears to be sneaking a glance. Getting the once-over is René Adorée. The film is A Certain Young Man. *Courtesy, MGM Studios*

Courtesy, Abbe Studios

gigantic production company to Italy. On arrival, Mussolini, who had enticed Metro with guarantees of unlimited cooperation, suddenly saw the great American dollar sign and applied multisided financial pressure on the program. Troubles with extras and unions and locals, inflated prices for props and liquor, interminable delays, troubles, troubles, troubles, and Metro finally disposed of the Italian footage and returned to Hollywood. "By the time they finish this one," remarked an extra, "Hollywood itself will be biblical history," but the cameras rolled on. When the film was released, Novarro appeared seminaked through a good portion of the first half (the original uncut version was filled with nudity, despite the fact that Will Hays's censorship board had called it "a wholesome, instructive and deeply religious epic"), and was such an enormous hit that for years afterwards letters addressed to "Mr. Ben Hur" arrived in his mailbox. This was in 1926. Four years later the talkies were upon him, and although his voice was adequate, the fans, hungry for total change, gave him thumbs down.

"I am selling personality," he said in 1931, when heads were rolling on every lot. "When I have lost vogue I have lost everything. Before it's too late I want to stop." The next year the lead story in a film magazine read, "I quit Goldwyn for yoga, says Ramon Novarro." "Yoga gives me the state of tranquility towards which we should all strive," he was quoted as saying, and added, "I think I am on the road toward attaining it." Whatever his real motives were, Novarro left the screen to tour abroad as an opera singer. The tour passed pleasantly enough, except for an incident in England when a careless stagehand in the flies dropped a sandbag on his head, knocking him out cold in the middle of an aria, and at the end of the tour he returned to Hollywood and settled down to a relatively quiet life.

Whatever the peculiar laws that govern entertainers, it is a strange fact that many of the biggest male screen stars have met tragic deaths. John Gilbert and Arthur Johnson died of drink, Wallace Reid of drugs, Barrymore of dissipation, Valentino of a ruptured ulcer, and so on. Perhaps the most terrible death was Novarro's. One evening in 1968 two men, the Ferguson brothers, forced their way into his home and bludgeoned him with a cane from one of his films. He died choking on his own blood. "With all his stage and screen experience," said a newspaper obituary, "it was ex-star Ramon Novarro's tragedy not to recognize two bad actors when he saw them."

The Public Loves of the Matinee Idol

JOHN GILBERT

From a hiding place somewhere in the hills, the great Garbo said no. No, she would not appear in the new movie MGM had scheduled for her. No, she would not perform as another *femme fatale*.

Even the name of the film, *Flesh and the Devil*, dripped of that lurid something that she detested, and for weeks Garbo remained in defiance of her contract. Then suddenly, without explanation, she came out of hiding and agreed to make the film. What had happened? No one was quite sure, but gossip was afoot. And gossip had it that the reason for her return was that dashing Jack Gilbert, a man she had admired from afar, was to be her leading man.

Greta Garbo and John Gilbert in a scene from Flesh *and the Devil. Courtesy, MGM Studios*

The love scenes between Gilbert and Garbo in *Flesh and the Devil* are among the greatest romantic sequences ever filmed, no doubt because they were real. During the shooting of these scenes —they were the first to feature open-mouthed kissing on screen— the two principals continued to embrace long after the director yelled "Cut!" "They are in a blissful state of love," said Clarence Brown, the director of the film, "that is so like a rosy cloud that they imagine themselves hidden behind it, beneath it." And *Photoplay* magazine, not to be outdone, claimed that "when John kissed Greta the audience felt like tiptoeing out as the lights came on in the theatre; they felt like peeping Toms."

Gilbert had fallen deeply in love with Garbo during the making of *Flesh and the Devil,* and it was said that she loved him too—at least for the fourteen days it took to shoot their scenes. Gilbert had a reputation as a cynical and frustrated man. He had come to Hollywood to direct and ended being directed in dozens of movies which he called "namby-pamby romances," an especially degrading medium for a man whose dream was to be a creative master of film. "Someday when my mind is more at ease and my soul no longer feels the need to search, as it does now," he told an interviewer, "I hope to write my own picture and play in it. Not until then shall I consider myself a creator, or artist, if you like."

Enter Miss Garbo to turn the potential artist into a panting satyr. Word of his infatuation with her spread across the land of moviedom as fast as a brush fire in the Hollywood hills. Fan magazines sizzled with the news. "Miss G., who is well known for her Viking coolness in affairs of the heart," said one of them, "has, we are told, been thawed to a pool of steaming hot water by the amorous attentions of that most popular of stars, Mr. John Gilbert."

Gilbert, however, had only recently merited being called "that most popular of stars." In films since 1915, he was never able to break away from character parts and secondary roles and found himself used and reused in dozens of frivolous light romances. Once, in rebellion, he quit films entirely and became a tire salesman, but soon he was back on his motley rounds, playing a Russian nobleman in *His Hour,* a bareback rider in *He Who Gets Slapped,* a schoolteacher in *The Snob,* and in *The Wife of a Centaur* the centaur himself. "They missed a great opportunity to make me a dinosaur in *The Lost World,*" he said as the obscurity of character roles weighed heavily on his ambitions, but in 1925 he attracted so much attention as the gallant Prince Danilo in a screen version

Doughboy Gilbert gives French belle, René Adorée, a piece of American chewing gum in a famous love scene from The Big Parade. *Courtesy, MGM Studios*

of Franz Lehar's operetta, *The Merry Widow,* that director King Vidor picked him for the lead in *The Big Parade.*

    The Big Parade was one of the earliest films about World War I, and one of the most successful. Gilbert played the doughboy, Jim Apperson, sent to fight in the trenches of France. There he meets Melisande, played by René Adorée. They fall in love. After a brief but ardent courtship he is ordered to the front and marches off, dragging Melisande behind him. When the war is over, finding his American girlfriend married to another man and his heart still on fire for Melisande, he returns to France to find her and they are reunited, vowing never to separate again. "What a buck private and what a lover!" cried the press books. "Those who see this wonderful doughboy woo the temperamental Melisande forget entirely that he is acting and think of him as a real flesh-and-blood character."

    There was some truth to this statement. There was something in the simple love story of a young American boy and a French peasant girl that captured the popular fancy, something in the heartrending scenes of their separation that caused people to cry, perhaps because they themselves were only five years removed from their own wartime romances and tragedies. It was not only the poignant theme of wartime love and separation, however, that captivated people. It was the enormous spectacle of the picture itself, which featured a cast of 2,500; few such ambitious productions had been attempted since *Intolerance* flopped at the box offices.

With the success of *The Big Parade* millions of adolescent victims of Gilbertmania across the nation begged the studios for more. Gilbert was named "The Perfect Lover" (as many before him had been and many after him would be), and soon took his place one step below Valentino as the most popular male actor in America.

In Hollywood Gilbert's prowess as an off-screen lover was already well known, and the gossip pages made much of the fact that it was a point of honor with him to conquer all his leading ladies. But Garbo, he told the world, was different. In her he claimed to see the little girl and the temptress, the handmaiden of the earth and the Eternal Mother. She, if not as articulate, was not immune to his advances, and made frequent trips to his flamboyant mansion in Beverly Hills.

Fire and ice, the papers called her. But whenever Jack proposed marriage she was quicksilver. "Oh, Jackie," she would say. "Oh, Jackie, but you are just a child."

He reacted to her rebuffs with ambivalence, now buying her a hundred thousand dollar yacht which she scarcely acknowledged, now ignoring her, now dragging her off to the justice of the peace in Santa Ana where she managed to escape his honorable intentions by hiding in the powder room. The relationship seesawed. Gilbert would announce their engagement; Garbo would deny it. Then Garbo grew bored with Gilbert's passion and petulance and ended the affair, announcing that she and Gilbert were just "good friends."

Although the story was clouded with the purple prose released by the press, one can guess why the relationship was ill-starred.

Garbo and Gilbert
Courtesy, MGM Studios

Perhaps no off-screen romance has ever caused such a sensation as the Gilbert-Garbo affair, and perhaps none ever received such coverage from the press. Here, on location for Flesh and the Devil, *Garbo and Gilbert were snapped in a reputedly candid moment, although such "unguarded" shots were usually staged for the occasion.*

Garbo was a natural hermit, mortifyingly shy, torn between a desire to perform and a hatred of the spotlight. Gilbert was her antithesis. He was extremely emotional, temperamental, consistently extroverted, a spendthrift, an insatiable wolf, a man once described as having enthusiasms as transient as newspaper headlines—in short, a child, "just a child."

Gilbert married the actress Ina Claire on the rebound and drank the relationship into divorce. Until 1929 he maintained his enormous popularity and was preparing to live out his dream of becoming a director. Then the talkies arrived. When Gilbert said, "I love you," the millions of women who had thrilled to his baritone gesticulations now discovered that his voice was a high, sissified tenor. By 1931 he was finished, the greatest casualty of the talkies. "From Garbo to limbo," said John Barrymore, his next-door neighbor.

John Gilbert then drank himself to death.

JOHN BARRYMORE

The last great film star to be called a matinee idol was John Barrymore. He was also the only actor to maintain this title through three different eras of show business—the stage, the silents, and the talking films. He was the embodiment of those traits that made the matinee idols outstanding: he was a match for the most urbane of tailored gentlemen (including his uncle, John Drew). As a swashbuckler in a costume piece he was unbeatable; some felt that as a Shakespearean actor he had no equal in the twentieth century; few comedians did such justice to pantomime, slapstick, and song and dance; and none was more accomplished at making love. He was everything the matinee idol could be, the final and most perfect statement of a type that had disappeared even before his own career was played out.

Barrymore started life as a commercial illustrator, but few magazines were buying. "I am in the theater because I failed at everything else," he wrote with the complacent frankness of an established man recounting his failures. "There is hope or at least money for an indifferent actor. An indifferent painter can only starve." Starving was not his fancy. He became a thespian, as his sister Ethel had done and as his brother Lionel would do, and from 1903 to the end of the decade he was a regular in romantic comedies.

His first chance at serious drama came in 1916 when he played William Falder, the defaulting clerk in John Galsworthy's *Justice*. Opening night on the road did not run smoothly. During his biggest scene, as he was being taken to a cell by brutal guards, he inadvertently leaned on the bars of the cage, which for stage purposes were made of wood, and smashed them to pieces. But, so the story is told, a press agent with the peculiar name of A. Toxen Worms, who had obviously been asleep through most of the performance, sent out glowing notices, claiming that "Barrymore's escape was the best thing in the weighty highbrow show." These

• 145

John Barrymore in Beloved Rogue.
Courtesy, United Artists

Four faces of John Barrymore. From left to right, at the beginning of his career, in costume for A Stubborn Cinderella *in 1909, as Hamlet in 1923, and in his forties. It is difficult to believe it is the same man in all four pictures.*

notices reached New York ahead of Barrymore and the critics were already biased in his favor. He was consequently an instant hit.

Exit the song-and-dance man and enter the romantic star. By 1917 the matinee idol was a sorry carbon of what he had once been, but in *Peter Ibbetson* Barrymore raised him from his death-bed. The play was written by George Du Maurier, creator of another matinee favorite, Svengali. It concerned a young man of great sensibility, Peter Ibbetson, who fell in love with a rich duchess. By some terrible accident he was condemned to life imprisonment, and

in his cell he visited the beloved duchess in his daydreams. *Peter Ibbetson* almost overloaded the emotional circuits of the feminine nervous system. Fifteen times during its run the curtain had to be brought down in the middle of a scene when sobbing drowned out the dialogue. One woman proudly announced she had seen the play forty-five times and cried on each occasion, and the plot was taken so seriously that committees were formed to improve conditions in men's prisons where, ostensibly, thousands of other Peter Ibbetsons were languishing. Once the show was canceled altogether when a woman was taken directly from the theater to the hospital with what was termed "an unaccountable weeping hysteria." The unfortunate woman was hospitalized for over two weeks.

Then came the serious dramas. In 1918 Barrymore did Tolstoy's *Redemption*; in 1919, *The Jest*; in 1920, *Richard III*; and in 1923, he played Hamlet 101 times, breaking Edwin Booth's record by one. The melancholy intellectualism of Barrymore's Hamlet fascinated New York. So did the incestuous inferences he introduced into the relationship between Hamlet and his mother, said by some to be based on an affair the actor reputedly had with his stepmother when he was fourteen. Critics compared him to Edwin Booth and Kean and even to Garrick himself. He was heralded as the greatest actor in America, and a jury of twelve women, some of them nationally famous, picked him as the second most fascinating man in the world, just behind the Duke of Wales. Few geniuses have ever been so lavishly rewarded for their talents. Theatergoers deemed him a god and waited in ecstatic expectation for his next Shakespearean triumph. It didn't come. In 1925 John Barrymore moved to Hollywood.

Barrymore's desertion startled the theater world more than it should have, for all the time he had been playing heavy drama in

Barrymore in The Sea Beast *with his wife-to-be, Dolores Costello, daughter of the actor, Maurice Costello. Courtesy, Warner Brothers*

New York he was making Chaplinesque farces on the coast. *The Incorrigible Dukane* was typical of these comedies. In it he was thrown, Keystone style, out of a saloon on his head, run over by a horse, knocked into a slag pile, attacked by a brutal mob, and pounded insensible with a lead pipe. For seven years he turned out these thigh-slappers, and in 1925 he went to Hollywood to stay.

He arrived with a fat contract from Warner Brothers and the right to approve all his stories, a luxury usually afforded only established screen stars. Warner's thought him worth it. They were still a small studio and would remain so until they introduced the talkies. Barrymore meant prestige, enough prestige to warrant paying him seventy-six thousand dollars a picture. He was a great catch, and was advertised as such: "John Barrymore, the greatest living actor," read the ad in *Variety*, "is now a Warner Brothers star."

The legitimate theater, of course, found it impossible to comprehend that Barrymore had forsaken his Shakespearean heritage for the meretricious allurements of Hollywood; and what's more, that he had done it with such relish, taking pot shots at the theater as he headed west. "The studio does away with the terrible repetition of a part," he wrote. "The screen is no less an art than the stage. The film has a different scope and I would say a broader one."

Barrymore's first movie as a citizen of California was *The Sea Beast,* a cinema version of *Moby Dick* with the character of Ahab altered just enough to make him the greatest Casanova of all time. Playing Ahab's inamorata in *The Sea Beast* was Dolores Costello, who would soon become his wife. "I laid eyes on that most preposterously lovely creature in the world," Barrymore once recounted. "She walked into the studio like a charming child, slender and shy and golden-haired. I knew that this was the one I had been waiting for."

Next came two period pieces, *Don Juan* and *Beloved Rogue,* both vintage Barrymore. He was already forty-four in 1926 and in a startlingly short time his famous "paper knife" profile would melt into jowls. But in *Beloved Rogue* he still looked the swain and made the best of it. He played François Villon, the medieval French poet, a philanthropic musketeer who shoots parcels of food to the starving people of Paris with the stingy Louis XI's own catapults and then shoots himself into Marceline Day's boudoir with the same contraption. "Every man has two souls," he tells her, "one for the world and one for the woman he loves." The malicious

Barrymore as François Villon in Beloved Rogue, *hiding from Thibault in Marceline Day's bedroom. Courtesy, Warner Brothers*

Thibault enters, takes her away, and tortures François until we are certain he has penned his last lines. But in the nick of time the king arrives to save him, all is well, and the unpleasant Thibault gets his just reward, a spanking from a dwarf.

It was really a throwback to the melodramatic theater, with a dash of Shakespearean technique thrown in, and audiences loved it. Many young filmgoers had never seen a real *actor* before, and they were astonished. A whimsical master of pantomime, Barrymore was capable of conveying all meanings through the medium of a quick glance, a faulty step, or a lifted brow. With a facial expression alone, he could make audiences cry; with a tilt of the head, he could make them laugh. He was a face actor, a hands and fingers actor; such subtlety was novel, especially in 1926 when physical overstatement was the norm. Although few realized it,

Barrymore was combining the traditional tricks he had learned on stage with modern cinematic method, emerging with his own special amalgam. This is why he had so few imitators, and unlike Valentino or Reid, never started a trend. Having skills that were unique, he was imposible to imitate.

Had he died then, at the end of the 1920's, when his eyes were still clear, he might be remembered as fondly as Valentino, still the perfect lover. But lives are remembered less for the way they begin than for the way they end. By the turn of that decade the advantage Barrymore had taken of all available depravities was showing in his physical deterioration, a decline made more pathetic by the very *publicness* of the whole thing. It was as if the gods, who had granted him everything a mortal might crave, were taking it all back, bit by bit, while he was yet on earth.

Barrymore and Greta Garbo in Grand Hotel. *Courtesy, MGM Studios*

Drunk on the set for *The Grand Hotel,* fluffing his lines, face bagging, temperamental fits, fist fights, all-night drunks, bottles piled in the bathtub, loss of memory, canceled contracts—by 1935 Barrymore was clearly sinking. A divorce from Dolores Costello ("she was too beautiful for words but not for arguments"), obscenities shouted at public functions, minor character parts parodying himself, chronic alcoholism and the same dementia that killed his father, bankruptcy, lawsuits, unemployment, two-week binges, trips to the sanitarium, crawling after producers for jobs, five-minute bits on soap operas—a terrible and heartbreaking pattern.

In 1940 they called him "The Clown Prince."

His career ended on a weekly radio program, Rudy Vallee's Fleishman's Yeast Hour. There his function was to serve as the target for endless jokes on himself, the classic, decrepit, washed-up ham.

"Say, did you hear shooting?"

"Oh, naw, that was just John Barrymore's knees cracking again."

Laughter.

In 1942 Barrymore lived alone in a mansion stripped of all its furniture except a bed and a chandelier. Finally, from a bad heart and liver inflamation, chronic alcoholism, ulcers, high blood pressure, a collapsed lung, and a possible brain tumor, John Barrymore passed away. "They can drag me through the courts of law," he told his critics shortly before he died, "flay me in the journals, and shout my name in the market places. But they cannot rob me of my dreams."

THE DEMISE OF THE MATINEE IDOL

The matinee idol lived through the silents, but he didn't survive the talkies. Times were changing. There were no more matinees, per se, of the talking films. Movie houses ran continuous performances which started at noon and went all day, and by the 1930's the concept of a single afternoon performance lost its significance. Furthermore, most of the remaining stage idols and silent screen lovers were no longer young. Neither were the fans who grew up with these men, and the generations that replaced them knew nothing of Saturday matinees. Just as other fashionable sobriquets such as "Arrow Collar man," "sheik," " 'it' girl," and "Gibson man" disappeared when they were no longer culturally relevant, so the term "matinee idol" disappeared when there were no more matinees and no more idols.

There were, of course, many more great male stars. But they were different now. The matinee idol, even though he played myriad different roles, was always and everywhere the *lover*. This was the essence of his function, to make love. It was his *raison d'être*. Women didn't come to watch him fight (the matinee idol fought only for a woman), or to dance (he rarely did), or to act (sometimes he could, sometimes he couldn't), or to seek adventure for its own sake (the idol quested only for love), or to push grapefruits into a woman's face (he would rather have died); they came, they waited, they watched, always, all the time, and only to see their idol make love.

The new male stars of the talkies were not *primarily* lovers. They were of course handsome, swaggering men, with plenty of romantic sequences in their films. Yet romance was only part of their purpose, and often subsidiary to the toughness, humor, boyishness or grace of the type they represented. For the new stars were *types* before they were *lovers*.

Talking pictures also witnessed the emergence of the man's actor. Valentino, Novarro, Gilbert, Bushman, all the biggest stars of the 20's were heir to the romantic stage tradition, and were primarily popularized by women. But in the 1930's, in the desperate dog days of the depression, men looked to the films for images of rough-and-ready heroes, heroes with the control over life they were denied, who laughed at the machinery that reduced the ordinary man to poverty and despair. They came to see Pat O'Brien defy the head command and fly his hazardous mission, Cagney knock the boss's daughter across the room and Robinson drill her with lead, Flynn laugh in the face of the black prince and tweak his nose, and Cooper take his quiet stand against ridiculous odds; they came to see the defiant Bogart, the stoic Tracy, the enthusiastic MacMurray, the man's man Gable; they came to see *men,* men of action, hard-riding, tight-fisted, no-nonsense men. No more hearts and flowers. That was women's stuff.

At the same time, the women were branching out in their popular affections. As they were fainting over the suave voices of men like Ronald Colman and a new line of Englishmen brought to Hollywood because they "knew how to speak," they were falling in love with a voice over the radio. Entertainers like Tony Wons, with his microphone-caressing tones, and Rudy Vallee, the "Vagabond Lover," kept millions of women chained to their radio sets. Vallee's popularity was due not to a great voice but an intimate voice that talked to women in their living rooms and their boudoirs. Then followed Crosby, the crooner brigades, the singing cowboys, the operetta men, the flashy male trios and quartets of the 40's, and by the time Sinatra's singles were the rage with bobby-soxers, the record business had become the big money. The voice alone was now a sex symbol.

By World War II the movies were at the height of their prosperity, but the times kept changing. The rough wartime screen actors gave way to the crewcut heroes, the teenage rebels and the flannel-suited executives of the 50's, and all gave way to television. Television killed the films as movies just as the films killed the theater; and as stars of the stage were once financially obliged to enter pictures, so picture stars now turned to TV. While television destroyed the cinematic star system, however, it did little to replace it, and in the twenty years of its reign it produced a sparse handful of major luminaries. By 1970 the only remaining stars of visual entertainment were, by an ironic turnabout, the directors. Now people no longer came to see a Grant film or a Gable film, they came to see the films of Fellini or Polanski or Truffaut.

While the star syndrome in films was collapsing a new one was preparing to replace it. The craze for male vocalists which started in the 30's and 40's with Vallee and Sinatra accelerated to cosmic speed with Elvis Presley and rock-and-roll, and reached its ultimate fulfillment in 1964 when the coming of the Beatles proclaimed the era of the rock singer. Out of the rock world came things strange and bizarre which would have made the matinee idol of an earlier year blush: hard-core sexuality incorporated into love lyrics, the reign of the ugly idol (Ringo Starr, Tiny Tim, Joe Cocker), acid rock and the music-drug culture, and with Mick Jagger and the Rolling Stones, the concept of unisex, and the introduction of the diabolical into the world of popular entertainment.

As the times change the forms of entertainment change, constantly reflecting the image and likeness of the civilization that creates them, and with each new change in the medium a change in the choice of popular idol takes place as well. Every newly evolved form of entertainment from the stage to the silents to the radio to the talkies to television to rock-and-roll to pop and folk and acid rock brings with it new requirements—and only those who can fill these requirements will become the stars of the times.

The modern idols with their modern obsessions, and the idols of all ages past, are men who fill collective needs, who give people something in the playhouse they can't find at home. "One might describe the theater, somewhat unaesthetically," wrote Carl Jung, "as an instutution for working out our private complexes in public." And this, perhaps, when all is said and done, is the explanation for the phenomenon that we chose to identify as the matinee idol.

INDEX

Action, man of, 101–102
Adams, Maude, 82
Adonis, 62
Adorée, René, 137, 141
After Dark, 69
Alimony, 125
All Story Weekly, 104
Always Audacious, 120–121
Anderson, Broncho Billy, 20, 107, 109
Anheuser-Busch Brewing Company, 98
Arab, The, 134, 136
Arbuckle, Fatty, 122
Archer, Belle, 57, 76
Arliss, George, 9, 100
Arrow Collar man, 116
Associated Press, 130
Autry, Gene, 113
Ayres, Agnes, 126

Baggot, King, 23, 87
Bancroft family, 10
Bara, Theda, 22
Barrymore, Ethel, 50, 145
Barrymore, John, 9, 17, 50, 138, 143, 145–52
Barrymore, Lionel, 9, 50, 145
Barrymore, Maurice, 48–51
Barthelmess, Richard, 115, 119, 126
Batman, 90
Battle, The, 65
Bayne, Beverly, 23, 86–89
Beatles, 155
Bellew, Kyrle, 9, 40–44
Beloved Rogue, 144, 149, 150
Ben Hur, 89, 107, 108, 136, 137
Bernhardt, Sarah, 50, 94
Bertha the Sewing Machine Girl, 65
Beverly, Edwin, 14

Big Bonanza, The, 73
Big Money, The, 129
Big Parade, The, 141–42
Bingham, Amelia, 54
Birth of a Nation, 100, 118
Black Pirate, 105
Blackwell, Carlyle, 23
Blood and Sand, 128
Blue, Monte, 133, 135
Blue Devil, The, 95
Bluebeard, 18
Bogart, Humphrey, 128, 154
Bohemian Club, 37
Booth, Edwin, 9, 31, 32, 147–48
Booth, John Wilkes, 31–35
Booth, Rachel, 57
Boucicault, Dion, 37–38, 43, 69
Bow, Clara, 133
Brady, William, 10, 38
Brian, Donald, 16, 17
Brisbane, Arthur, 89
Broken Seal, The, 78
Brown, Clarence, 140
Bunny, John, 9
Busher, The, 119
Bushman, Francis X., 23, 85–90, 107, 154
Butterflies, 73

Cagney, James, 128, 154
Camille, 45, 125, 128
Captain Swift, 50–51
Caruso, E., 93
Cashel Byron's Profession, 69
Castle, Irene, 74
Castle, Vernon, 74
Certain Young Man, A, 137
Chaplin, Charles, 98

Cherry, Charles, 23
Chicago *Tribune*, 130
Cinderella, 18
Cinema vérité, 108
Civil War, 10, 33
Claire, Ina, 143
Clapp, William, 29
Clark, George, 72
Clodhopper, The, 119
Cocker, Joe, 155
Coghlan, Charles, 75
Coghlan, Rose, 56, 75
Cohan, George M., 100
Coleridge, Samuel Taylor, 28
Collier's Weekly, 85
Colman, Ronald, 75, 154
Combination companies, 11–12
Conquering Power, The, 125
Cooper, Gary, 154
Corbett, James J., 68–69
Cortez, Ricardo, 133, 135
Costello, Dolores, 149, 152
Costello, Maurice, 19, 22
Count of Monte Cristo, The, 14, 46
Cowboys, 107–13
Crosby, Bing, 154
Curry, Jim, 51
Curse of Capistrano, The, 104

Daly, Augustin, 50, 72
Davenport, E. L., 38, 70
Davenport, Fanny, 70–72
Davis, Jefferson, 34
Davis, Richard Harding, 85
Davy Crockett, 46–47
Day, Marceline, *150*
De Mille, Cecil B., 85
Dempsey, Jack, 103
De Pixerécourt, Guilbert, 14
Depression, 154
Dickens, Charles, 45
Diplomacy, 10, 51
Dixey, Henry, 62–64
Don Juan, 149
Don Q. Son of Zorro, 105
Dos Passos, John, 129
Double Speed, 118
Doubleday, Abner, 75
Drew, Georgie, 49
Drew, John, 49, 72–75, 145
DuCrow, Tote, 98
Duelling, 76–79
Dumas, Alexandre (fils), 13, 45
Du Maurier, George, 65, 146
Duncan, Isadora, 93
Dyas, Ada, 37

Eagle, The, 125
East Lynne, 22
Edison, T. A., 18, 87
Eisenhower, Dwight, 103

Emerson, John, 101
Emerson and Hooley's Minstrel Show, 59
Essanay Film Studios, 23–24, 86, 89
Excuse My Dust, 118

Fads, 129
Fairbanks, Douglas, 20, 32, 96–105, 126
Famous Players, 118
Farrar, Geraldine, 95
Faversham, William, 80–82
Fechter, Charles, 45–46
Fedora, 70, 72
Ferguson brothers, 138
Fitzgerald, F. Scott, 113
Fitzsimmons, Bob, 68
Fleishman's Yeast Hour, 152
Flesh and the Devil, 139, 143
Flynn, Errol, 154
Four Horsemen of the Apocalypse, The, 124, 125
Frenzied Finance, 100
Frisky Mrs. Johnson, The, 65
Frohman, Charles, 12, 79, 81
Frohman, Daniel, 72
Fund drives, 98

Gable, Clark, 128, 154
Galsworthy, John, 145
Garbo, Greta, 139–43
Garrick, David, 148
Gentleman Jim, 69
Gentleman of France, A, 44
Gentlemen Prefer Blondes, 101
Gerish, Sylvia, 74
Gibson, Charles Dana, 85
Gibson, Hoot, 113
Gibson man, 85
Gilbert, John, 38, 135, 137, 138, 139–43, 154
Gish, Lillian, 20
Goldwyn, Samuel, 95
Grand Hotel, 151, 152
Great Secret, The, 23
Great Train Robbery, The, 18, 107, 109
Griffith, D. W., 19, 100
Gush columns, 15

Hackett, James H., 76
Hackett, James K., 76–79
Haggard, H. Rider, 82
Hamilton, Neil, *115*, *116*
Hamlet, 45
Hari, Mata, 93
Harron, Bobby, 23
Hart, William S., 107–13, 122
Hawk, Harry, 34
Hays, Will, 138
He Who Gets Slapped, 140
Heston, Charlton, 90
High Noon, 113

His Hour, 140
His Majesty the American, 100
Hollywood dream, 105
Holt, Jack, 115, 118, 122, 126
Home, 119
Honest Blacksmith, The, 68
Honest Hearts and Willing Hands, 68
Hopper, De Wolf, 100
Horror roles, 65–66
Howells, William Dean, 64
Hugo, Victor, 14

Ibáñez, Blasco, 125
Imogene, 56
Incorrigible Dukane, The, 149
Intolerance, 142
Irving, Henry, 42

Jagger, Mick, 155
Jansen, Marie, 55
Jazz Age, 103
Jeffries, Jim, 89
Jerome, Jerome K., 13
Jest, The, 147
Johnson, Arthur, 20–22, 138
Jung, Carl, 155
Justice, 145

Kalem Company, 137
Kean, Edmund, 9, 11, 24, 27–31, 35, 148
Kelcey, Herbert, 75
Kerrigan, J. Warren, 23, 87
Kerry, Norman, 124, 133, 135
King Lear, 65
Kinetoscopes, 18
Kiss Me Again, 133

Lackaye, Wilton, 65–66
Laemmle, Carl, 20
Lamb, The, 101
Lamb's Club, 49
Lampoons, 62–64
La Rocque, Rod, 135
Lasky, Jesse, 118–19
Latin types, 132–33
Lawrence, Florence, 20
Lee, Agnes, 54
Lehar, Franz, 141
Lessing, Madge, 53
Lester, Louise, 55
Life, 42
Life of an American Fireman, The, 18
Lincoln, Abraham, 31, 34
Lindbergh, Charles, 103
Lloyd, Harold, 9
Loos, Anita, 101
Lost World, The, 140
Love Special, The, 118
Lust for Gold, 95

Macbeth, 72
MacMurray, Fred, 154
Mantell, Robert, 20, 70–72
Maria Rosa, 95
Mark of Zorro, The, 104–105
Marriage Market, The, 16
Mash letters, 15
Mashers, 15
Mathis, June, 125
Matinee girl, 15–16
"Matinee idol," as a term, 10
Matinee money, 15
Matinees, origin of, 10
Mayer, Louis B., 89
Maynard, Ken, 113
Mayo, Edwin, 47
Mayo, Frank, 46–47
Meighan, Thomas, 115, 116, 121
Méliès, Georges, 18
Melodrama, 12–14, 76
Mencken, H. L., 130
Merchant of Venice, The, 27, 71
Merry Widow, The, 141
Metro Goldwyn Mayer (MGM), 137–38, 139
Midgleys, the, 74
Miller, Henry, 79–80
Minstrel shows, 59
Mix, Tom, 110–13
Moby Dick, 149
Modjeska, Madame, 49, 50
Mollycoddle, The, 102
Money Mad, 65
Monsieur Beaucaire, 129
Montague, Harry, 10, 35–40, 41, 43, 51
Moore, Tom, 23
Moreno, Antonio, 135
Morgan, J. Pierpont, 98
Morris, Clara, 32
Motion Picture Producers and Distributors League, The, 122
Murdock, Frank, 46
Mussolini, Benito, 138
Mutual Studios, 107

Nadjeska, 50
Nagel, Conrad, 122
Nazimova, 100, 125, 128
Negri, Pola, 127, 130
New York *Herald,* 33
Nickelodeons, 18, 19
Niven, David, 75
Nizam of Hyderabad, 42
Novarro, Ramon, 9, 89–90, 132–38, 154

O'Brien, Pat, 154
Olcott, Chauncey, 59–62
Old Swimmin' Hole, The, 119

Olivier, Laurence, 95
Omar, the Tentmaker, 132
O'Neill, Eugene, 46
O'Neill, James, 46
Othello, 28, 31
Our American Cousin, 34

Parker, Fess, 47
Peter Ibbetson, 146–47
Photoplay, 140
Pickford, Mary, 20, 103–105
Piton, Augustus, 59
Pollard, Herbert, 85
Ponisi, Elizabeth, 38
Porter, Ben, 51
Porter, Edwin, 18
Post, Guy Bates, 132
Potter, Cora, 42
Presley, Elvis, 155
Prisoner of Zenda, The, 76, 78–79
Prizefighters, 68–69
Publicity, 12, 86

Queen Elizabeth, 94
Queen of the Moulin Rouge, 86

Rambova, Natacha, 130
Rappe, Virginia, 122
Ray, Charles, 115, 119, 121, 126
Reaching for the Moon, 101
Record of the Boston Stage, 29
Red Riding Hood, 18
Redemption, 147
Rehan, Ada, 73
Reid, Hal, 118
Reid, Wallace, 113–22, 126, 138, 151
Repertory groups, 11
Rhodes, Thomas, 98
Richard III, 29, 30, 147
Rise of Silas Lapham, The, 64
Roaring Road, 118
Robin Hood, 105
Robinson, Edward G., 154
Robson, Eleanor, 43
Rock-and-roll, 155
Rodin, Auguste, 91
Rogers, Roy, 113
Rolling Stones, 155
Romance of a Poor Young Man, The, 38
Romance of the Dells, A, 89
Romantic drama, 13–14
Romeo and Juliet, 38, 43, 82
Roosevelt, Franklin, 90
Rue Prairie, 98
Rush seats, 15
Russell, Lillian, 16, 64

Salisbury, Jane, 132
Salvini, Tommaso, 32

Sardou, V., 10, 51, 72, 93
Scanlon, W. J., 59–60
Screen Actors' Guild, 90
Sea Beast, The, 148, 149
Selig Film Company, 111, 118
Serai, Louis, 78
Shane, 113
Shaughraun, The, 37
Shaw, Bernard, 69
She, 82
Sheik, The, 125, 131, 135
"Sheiks," 126
Shenandoah, 65, 79
Sherman, Lowell, 66
Sinatra, Frank, 154, 155
Snob, The, 140
Snow, Marguerite, 89
Soap operas, 77
Soldier of Fortune, 85
Soloman, Fred, 74
Sothern, E. H., 76, 78
Star system, 11–12
Starr, Ringo, 155
Stonehouse, Ruth, 89
Stubborn Cinderella, A, 146
Sullivan, John L., 68
Swordfighting thrillers, 76

Taking Chances, 95
Taming of the Shrew, 103
Television, 154–55
Tellegen, Lou, 91–96
Terry, Alice, 137
Thackeray, W. M., 10
Theatre, 15, 44, 117
Thief of Bagdad, The, 105
Three Musketeers, The, 14, 105
Tim, Tiny, 155
Tol'able, David, 119
Too Much Speed, 118
Tracy, Spencer, 154
Triangle Studios, 100–101, 107
Trilby, 65–66
Tumbleweeds, 112, 113

Uncle Tom's Cabin, 42
Under the Gaslight, 50
Union Club, 98
Universal Pictures, 20

Valentino, Rudolph, 39, 90, 113, 122–30, 138, 150, 154
Vallee, Rudy, 152, 154, 155
Vanity Fair, 10
Variety, 149
Victorian ethic, 35
Vidor, King, 141
Village Sleuth, The, 119
Vocalists, male, 59–62, 155

Wallace, Lew, 108
Wallack, Henry, 38
Walthall, Henry B., 23
Warner Brothers, 149
Washington *Times*, 89
Watch My Speed, 118
West, Benjamin, 29
Western films, 107–13
What's Your Hurry, 118
"When Johnny Comes Marching Home," 98
Who's Who, 77

Wife of a Centaur, The, 140
Wilbur, Crane, 87
Wilson, Woodrow, 104
Winter, William, 73
Women Have Been Kind, 91
Wons, Tony, 154
Wood, William, 11
World War I, 98, 117
World War II, 154
Wyndham, Sir Charles, 31, 32

Zucker, Adolph, 77

THE END